RETHINKING THE BUSINESS MODELS OF BUSINESS SCHOOLS: A CRITICAL REVIEW AND CHANGE AGENDA FOR THE FUTURE

RETHINKING THE BUSINESS MODELS OF BUSINESS SCHOOLS: A CRITICAL REVIEW AND CHANGE AGENDA FOR THE FUTURE

BY

KAI PETERS
Coventry University Group, Coventry, UK

RICHARD R. SMITH
Lee Kong Chian School of Business, Singapore Management University, Singapore

HOWARD THOMAS
Lee Kong Chian School of Business, Singapore Management University, Singapore

United Kingdom – North America – Japan – India – Malaysia – China

Emerald Publishing Limited
Howard House, Wagon Lane, Bingley BD16 1WA, UK

First edition 2018

British Library Cataloguing in Publication Data
A catalogue record for this book is available from the British Library

ISBN: 978-1-78754-875-6 (Print)
ISBN: 978-1-78754-874-9 (Online)
ISBN: 978-1-78754-876-3 (Epub)

ISOQAR certified
Management System,
awarded to Emerald
for adherence to
Environmental
standard
ISO 14001:2004.

Certificate Number 1985
ISO 14001

INVESTOR IN PEOPLE

Contents

Acknowledgements

This book would not have come into being without the collaboration, stimulus and support from a number of people, and of professional organisations.

Strong support has come from funding provided by EFMD (The European Foundation for Management Development) and GMAC (The Graduate Management Admissions Council). In particular, Eric Cornuel, Director General of EFMD and Sangeet Chowfla, President and CEO of GMAC, became the catalysts for a project examining not only pathways in the global evolution of management education, particularly in Africa and Latin America, but also the need for innovation in the business models of management schools globally. Helpful advice in this effort has also been given by Matthew Wood, Director of Operations at EFMD, and Ron Sibert, Director for Africa at GMAC and Dan Le Clair, COO at AACSB.

Among collaborators and contributors to this project it is important to recognise the generosity and openness of Deans and faculty colleagues. For example, Andrew Pettigrew of Said Business School, Oxford and Ken Starkey of Nottingham University have urged the importance of undertaking research studies on the evolution of global management education and on the adaptation of business school models to different cultures, contexts and countries. Further, Deans and strong friends, such as Michel Patry (HEC, Montreal), David Schmittlein (MIT Sloan), and Ken Freeman (Questrom School, Boston University) in North America; Peter Lorange (CEIBS, Europe), Santiago Iniguez (IE, Madrid, Spain), Jordi Canals (IESE, Barcelona, Spain) and Simon Collinson (Birmingham, UK) in Europe; Nicola Kleyn (GIBS, South Africa). Nick Binedell (GIBS, South Africa), Enase Okenedo (Lagos, Nigeria) and Thami Gorfi (ESCA, Morocco) in Africa; and finally Gaby Alvarado (ITAM, Mexico) and Fernando D'Alessio (Centrum) in Latin America deserve special thanks and gratitude. We would also like to thank colleagues and former doctoral students such as Amanda Goodell (Cass), Alex Wilson (Loughborough) and Julie Davies (Huddersfield).

However, it is also extremely important to recognise the considerable institutional and personal support provided by Singapore Management University. Howard is director of ASMEU (The Academic Strategy and Management Education Unit) at SMU, which has provided research assistance, data analysis and administrative support to this project. Beyond that, Professor Arnold de Meyer, President of SMU has mentored and given advice in his inimitable, quiet, effective leadership style. His long-term friendship is much appreciated by Howard.

At SMU, we also owe a debt of thanks to many other colleagues such as Professor Gerard George, Dean of LKCSB, Gregor Halff, Deputy Dean of LKCSB, and Professor Michelle Lee who is a co-author of Howard's papers and books about the evolution of global management education. We want to thank the research assistants, and especially Kashish Nain Israni, Geng Yun Sham, and Samantha Wong involved with this project. And our sincere appreciation goes to Jes Ong, Howard's PA, for assisting and managing the many stages and revisions that occurred as the project came to a successful conclusion.

We would also like to thank a number of individuals in the Ashridge/Hult ecosystem who have contributed through support in time or support intellectually over the years. A special thanks goes to Steve Hodges at Hult and Narendra Laljani and Martin Lockett who were Ashridge colleagues and co-authors for many years. Additionally, thanks must go to John Latham and other new colleagues at Coventry University who are disrupting not only the business school, but the overall university landscape.

Finally, the quality and readability of this book's contents is largely due to the professionalism of our consulting editor at EFMD, George Bickerstaffe along with our reference editor, Shirley James. However, we are solely responsible for the book's argument. We sincerely hope that it provides some insights and stimulates thinking about future directions and innovations in management education.

Kai Peters, Richard R. Smith, and Howard Thomas

About the Authors

Kai Peters is the Pro-Vice-Chancellor of Business and Law at the Coventry University Group in Coventry, U.K. Prior to joining Coventry, he served as CEO of Ashridge and the Chief Academic Officer at Hult International Business School. In addition to extensive management expertise in Business Schools, Kai serves on supervisory and advisory boards for a number of organizations in the academic and health care sectors. Kai is frequent speaker on the topic management education and the co-author of *Steward Leadership: A Maturational Perspective* and a board member of Centrepoint, a London-based charity for homeless youth.

Richard R. Smith is a Professor of Strategic Management (Practice) and Associate Dean for General Management Programmes at Lee Kong Chian School of Business, Singapore Management University. Prior to academic roles, Rick served as a Partner and Managing Director at Accenture in the USA, Hong Kong, and Singapore. He serves on the boards of the Singapore Government Civil Service College, QUEST-the global leadership institute for women, and the International Consortium for Executive Development and Research. Rick is a co-author of *Human Capital and Global Business Strategy* and a frequent speaker on strategic human capital and leadership for competitive advantage.

Howard Thomas is the LKCSB Distinguished Professor of Strategic Management, Lee Kong Chain School of Business, Director of the Academic Strategy and Management Education Unit, Singapore Management University, and the inaugural Ahmass Fakahany Distinguished Visiting Professor at Boston University Questrom School of Business. As former business school dean in four schools in four continents and a highly cited scholar, Howard continues to serve the academic community through his roles and fellowships in organizations such as AACSB, GMAC, SMS, GFME, and EFMD. Howard is the author of more than 30 books and one of the foremost authorities on management education around the world.

Preface

This book is the result of a strong collaboration and friendship between three business school professors with different experiences in, and perspectives on, the field of management education.

Howard Thomas comes from a more scholarly, academic tradition and career path. A lifelong academic, he has also been a Dean on three continents, namely, Europe, North America and Asia-most recently as Dean at the Lee Kong Chian School of Business in Singapore Management University (SMU). He has also chaired many organisations in the management education field such as CABS (UK), AACSB and GMAC (US), and EFMD (Europe). Howard is active in business as a board member, advisor, and speaker. He is also acknowledged as a highly cited scholar in the fields of strategic management and management education.

From a more applied academic tradition, Kai Peters has embraced both a successful corporate career at IBM and Volkswagen and broad international experience as a Dean at Erasmus University in Rotterdam, as Chief Executive at Ashridge Business School (UK) and as Chief Academic Officer at Hult International Business School. He is currently the Pro-Vice-Chancellor of Business and Law at Coventry University Group in the U.K. He serves on a variety of boards in the academic and health care sectors. Kai is also known as one of the top 100 HR professionals in the UK. He has an enviable reputation as a scholar and leader in the management education field.

In an even more practical vein, Rick Smith has had a highly successful business and consulting career in the USA, China, and Singapore. He served as a Senior Vice President in the Manpower Group, CEO of SSI Asia Pacific Limited, and Managing Director at Accenture. He serves on a variety of boards including the management development think-tank, ICEDR and the Singapore government's Civil Service College. After retiring from business, he transitioned to academia as an Associate Dean for Postgraduate Professional Programmes and Professor of Strategy Practice at SMU. His research interests are in corporate governance and strategic human capital.

Our overarching aim has been to draw on our wide-ranging experience of management education at all levels to explain and understand, from a value - based perspective, the existing business and teaching models currently adopted in business schools. More importantly, we examine the need for ongoing innovation in these models given the challenges of such factors as technology enabled learning, competition and disruption.

We also believe quite strongly that business schools must continually address their legitimacy, identity and value in the context of higher education. Dialogue and debate should continue about the potential role of business schools as professional schools like those in schools of engineering, law or medicine. Such schools would provide society with a cadre of responsible, reflective and insightful professional managers possessing a strong ethical and moral compass.

We hope our arguments provide insights and challenges for management educators. As a consequence, we look forward to your comments, criticisms and constructive feedback.

Kai Peters, Richard R. Smith, Howard Thomas

Introduction

By any standard, and despite many critical attacks, business schools are one of the success stories of higher education − if only in terms of their sheer growth in recent years. The Association for the Advancement of Collegiate Schools of Business (AACSB) estimates that there are more than 13,000 institutions in the world offering business degrees (The Economist, 2011) and the magazine also posits that there are between 1,500 and 2,500 business schools in India alone, making one wonder how a figure of 13,670 is arrived at with any degree of accuracy (The Economist, 2011). Whether this number is a correct estimate of market size or not, it really only includes the number of institutions that award their own degrees. Many institutions offer degrees provided by other degree-awarding institutions. Indeed, the British Council estimates that there are over 700,000 students outside the UK studying for validated UK degrees. In addition, Australian, New Zealand and Canadian schools are also in the validation business and thus also contribute to the overall increase in business degree provision.

Given the number is undoubtedly large, some attempt to provide consumer advice, guidance and differentiation is offered by accreditations and rankings. AACSB accredits nearly 800 schools worldwide. The EFMD's European Quality Improvement System (EQUIS) about 170 schools and the Association of MBAs (AMBA) 245 programmes. These numbers continue to grow as the international footprint of business schools increases (Urgel, 2007). At the time of writing (Summer 2017), 76 schools appear to be accredited by all three of the above associations. Many of the triple-accredited schools cite that they are in the "top 1% of business schools world-wide", which probably sounds better than saying they are in the "top half-a-percent" worldwide. Accreditation is becoming increasingly important as a means of providing some market transparency and comparison as entrants jostle into the business of management education and established schools become increasingly globalised (Trapnell, 2007).

Rankings provide a second well-known guide to the business school landscape. Most of the major rankings providers (often media-based organisations) restrict themselves to making lists of 100 top schools and a smaller number of schools in the executive education rankings. One organisation, Eduniversal, attempts the Herculean (and hardly scientific) task of providing a ranking of the top 1,000 schools worldwide. However, rankings are, rightly or wrongly, often perceived as highly manipulated and often unfairly re-levelled based on changing sets of criteria (Corley and Gioia, 2000).

The overall growth in business school numbers can be attributed to several factors. The most obvious is that for the students who attend business school business education tends to be positively correlated with getting a good job. A second factor is simply that the world has become more of a business-oriented marketplace. A whole host of business schools were formed or reformed following the 1989 fall of the Berlin Wall and related events in most Eastern European countries. In other parts of the world, notably across Asia, rapid industrialisation has also prompted the growth in business schools as has market-oriented liberalisation in China. A third factor is perhaps more self-serving from the schools' side. Providing business education, a "chalk and talk" subject that does not require such expensive infrastructure as medicine or engineering do, is seen as a (potential) cash cow. Certainly, if one focuses on teaching, foregoing research and working mainly with adjuncts and practitioners as faculty, the cost base can be kept relatively low.

Many business education providers do not grant degrees at all and focus specifically on executive education. If estimating the size of the degree-granting market is a challenge, working out the size of the executive education provider market overall is next to impossible. Non-degree business education includes all manner of providers ranging from business schools themselves to specialist providers, to the major consultants and HR service providers, to boutiques to single business operators.

Khurana (2007) writes that in the mid-1950s there were only 150 universities in the US that offered business degrees and that the US provided the bulk of business degrees world-wide at that time. Growth since then has been extraordinary and the market-place, while internationalising and reaching out to new populations previously not served by business education, has also become more crowded in pretty well every market around the world.

Reflections on the Business School Environment

Business schools around the world have examined and commented on a world in flux for the past several decades. They watched, and often encouraged, the neo-liberal dismantling of state-run industries in the 1980s and 1990s (and continuing to this day) as they were thrown open to competition. While in many cases competition ensured that organisations were better run, in other cases it led to former public utilities being required by regulators to offer historical services. For example, residual post offices might be required to deliver postcards to the remote Orkney Islands or to Alaska in January at regulated prices. New competitors, unsurprisingly, avoided these uneconomic legacy services in favour of delivering packages between metropolitan hubs where lucrative and low-hanging profits could be harvested. Historical labour arrangements, pension and health care promises and often unionisation were avoided. New models sought to arbitrage specific opportunities in long-established integrated and cross-subsidised value chains.

More recently, business schools watched excitedly as Schumpeterian disruption rapidly reconfigured entire industries. Driven by the combined forces of globalisation and technological innovation, traditional retailing has been usurped by online shopping; digital culture − music, films and books − has undergone a similar upheaval; and taxi and hotel business models have been challenged by new providers of travel and accommodation. For Uber and AirBnB in the western world, there is a host of fast-following competitors across Asia, Africa and Latin America.

Over the past few years, business schools have hosted conferences and faculty have written articles and case studies about these changes − as they should. Our own institutions run academic and practitioner conferences on the multi-generational workforces. As lives get longer, we must take into account the needs of the millennial generation certainly. But we must also come to terms with an ageing workforce that needs to continue to work well past traditional retirement ages as once sacrosanct promises of adequate pension and health care provision are reduced.

Conferences on global disruption and organisational responses have taken note of a world of volatility, uncertainty, complexity and ambiguity (VUCA) where droughts, floods and other environmental disturbances lead to refugee crises and population displacement.

Technological changes as well as the shifting of economic growth from traditional Western powers to the rapidly developing economies of

China and India and the southern hemisphere have led to new questions of dissatisfied populations and self-serving national agendas.

These changes and global events provide management scholars with ample topics to explore in research, writing and teaching. But while the world of business has been changing dramatically, the world *inside* the business school continues in the same manner and tradition as it has for decades.

Since the turn of the millennium, and certainly in the period following the great crash of 2007/2008, graduating students have switched their career goals from a job in investment banking and prestigious consultancies to joining "cool" technology companies, internet-based start-ups, social media plays, games and niche retailing. Observing these trends from inside, traditional business schools have generally not been inclined to disrupt their own models of delivery. Yes, there are on-line courses and other changes around the periphery but the core business of business schools remains relatively static. This begins to raise questions over the legitimacy and impact of business schools in today's fast-paced business environment (Pettigrew and Starkey, 2016).

Business schools have, it must be noted, regularly tried to turn the mirror on themselves. Each of the major global business school associations regularly run conferences on themes such as the AACSB's 2016 Deans conference on "Innovations that Inspire"; and the theme for 2017 was "Can business schools be the leading catalysts for innovation and new business creation?" The EFMD's 2016 Deans and Directors conference was themed "Business Schools: Purpose in Context". The subsequent 2017 conference in Ljubljana, Slovenia, was entitled "Leading in a world of uncertainty". Similarly, themed events are regularly organised by GMAC, AMBA, CABS in the UK and similar organisations bringing together deans and senior managers from business schools around the world.

At the end of the day, however, as the 2011 report of the AACSB International's Globalization of Management Education Task Force notes in *Globalization of Management Education: Changing International Structures, Adaptive Strategies, and the Impact on Institutions*, business schools have been slow to take disruption seriously: "…compared to the business environment, higher education tends to be more tightly rooted in tradition, and tends to encounter more inertia than business in the face of change" (AACSB, 2011, p.13).

This trend to highlight conference themes as calls to action to business schools goes much further back than 2011. In the seminal 1988 book, *Management Education and Development: Drift or Thrust into the*

21st Century, Porter and McKibbin, commissioned by AACSB to write a book compiling and contextualising a three-year study on the state of business education, noted in their introduction:

> "The study is unique in that it not only looks at management education as traditionally delivered through colleges and universities, but also focuses on other educational delivery systems, such as corporations, and third-party providers, which the earlier conference reports predicted would play an increasingly significant role in the years ahead as knowledge bases continue to grow and demands to enlarge the business school curriculum increase, the relationships among these three (types of) providers and decisions about who should teach what become more important than ever before."

Overview of the Book

The goal of this book is to explore these issues and questions about the future of business schools. To date there has been thoughtful analysis and soul-searching by deans but not necessarily a lot of direct action or reaction by business schools. The aim here is to deconstruct and reconstruct the multiple value chains of business education across the extensive spectrum of business school activities. Breaking business school behaviours into stages in their various chains means unashamedly wearing managerial hats and looking at how the broad activities of business schools operate. This involves looking at income streams and at service providers, who affect what we do, how we do it and what we genuinely need to consider in the short, not the long, term.

Whether they like it or not the vast majority of business schools need to be aware of the market. With the exception of a fortunate few, almost all business schools cannot fall back on state guarantees nor extensive endowments for their financial viability and future success. Business schools are businesses and this book is about the "business of business schools".

Structurally, the book is straightforward, beginning in Chapter 1 with an overview of the extensive literature about and around business schools though it notes that there is surprisingly little about the theme of this book, the business of business schools.

Many elements and perspectives exist. In fact, there has been a boom in writing about business schools in recent years. However, much of the analysis is based on observation coupled with a fair amount of criticism and hand-wringing. Whereas Porter and McKibbin, writing in 1988, state that their "report documents the first systematic study of its type in over 25 years and exemplifies an internally generated evaluation of management education, as compared to the externally driven Ford and Carnegie report of the late 1950s" published output in the period since 1988 and certainly since the turn of the millennium has been profuse.

Chapters 2 and 3 propose and develop the various value chains operating within business schools. Not all value chains exist in every school but every school has a number of value chains with different challenges and opportunities. As one of the present authors was told by a trustee, "Your school is more complicated than a multinational organisation." This book provides a simple value chain analysis for the various "product offerings" of a business school including undergraduate degrees, pre-experience postgraduate programmes, the MBA, the Executive MBA and executive education. Outsiders often view business education as a simple process but deconstructing each of these offerings illustrates the synergies as well as the large differences in each. Challenges that are seemingly unrelated to education such as housing, meals, transport and other such services have become integral to many management education offerings in recent years as well as other trends driving the challenges and competitive issues that many business schools face today.

We also describe and analyse new entrants, or third-party providers, who are clearly seeking to achieve economic success in their interactions with the business education market. There is no attempt to present an entire overview of all new providers or alternative provision that exists; this is not a market study. But it does seek to be more a typology of players illustrated with examples rather than a holistic overview, which would be thankless and impossible in a fast-moving environment.

Chapters 4 and 5 explore the value proposition of business schools and the associated implications on their financial models. Considering the business of running a business school starts with the value proposition that immediately shows a clear bifurcation of interests.

On one hand is a traditional university orientation that proposes providing education for students in a way that creates human capital to benefit society. This society-based orientation generally reflects a strong fit with government funding in support of the associated economic benefits.

On the other hand, is a strong return on investment (ROI) orientation as a value proposition for management education. As an example, potential MBA students are often found calculating the anticipated future returns (high salaries and career prospects) against the high costs (fees, housing and opportunity cost) of attending a full-time MBA programme. This ROI-based value proposition has significant implications for business schools as it creates a foundation for increased competition with clear implications on the financial model. The ongoing debate of offering programmes that are immediately relevant to business *vs* finding ways to expand the horizons of comprehension of students can weigh heavily as educators consider curriculum and offerings (Chia, 2014).

In addition to considering the sources of financial income for a business school, the book looks in detail at the income streams within a business school in significant detail and through various lenses − in the round, per activity, per student and per faculty member. In response to the changing nature of management education, it also introduces a potentially controversial model that we call a "revenue delivered view" of measuring contributions and aligning efforts toward the profitability outcomes. As is noted, the increasing pressure and orientation on margins in business schools is starting to shift the competitive landscape.

Chapters 6 and 7 look at how business schools might consider future uncertainty in the external marketplace while also striving for innovation driven by internal capability. Addressing these areas begins by examining what the literature tells us about future leadership needs in driving innovation. Just as our own scholars discuss the critical role of the CEO and top management teams, business schools must take note of their own future leaders and leadership teams in the light of anticipated dilemmas that future business school deans will need to address related to the internal innovation and management of their schools.

The external business and management education marketplace is changing rapidly as new extensions, acquisitions, mergers and alliances take shape. This is particularly true with stand-alone private business schools. As new models for management education continue to evolve, so too do the players, models and partnerships. Different forms of competitive advantage lead to an examination of both the drivers for mergers and acquisitions within the sector as well as to case examples of new constellations of the value chain.

The book's conclusion is a synthesis that fully recognises and values the tremendous contributions that business education and business schools provide for their students and society at large blended with a call to arms that we practise what we preach. We have been a part of the tremendous growth and success with business schools around the world over the last few decades. Looking forward we see the signs that our own industry is poised for disruption. We hope that our collective efforts will contribute to how we might manage our affairs well into the future as stewards of business schools.

References

AACSB International. (2011). *Globalization of management education: Changing international structures, adaptive strategies, and the impact on institutions* (Report of the AACSB International Globalization of Management Education Task Force).

Chia, R. (2014). From relevance to relevate: How university-based business school can remain seats of "higher" learning and still contribute effectively to business. *Journal of Management Development, 33*(5), 443–455.

Corley, K., & Gioia, D. (2000). The rankings game: Managing business school reputation. *Corporate Reputation Review, 3*(4), 319–333.

Khurana, R. (2007). *From higher aims to hired hands: The social transformation of American business schools and the unfulfilled promise of management as a profession.* Princeton, NJ: Princeton University Press.

Pettigrew, A., & Starkey, K. (2016). From the Guest Editors: The legitimacy and impact of business schools—Key issues and a research agenda. *Academy of Management Learning & Education, 15*(4), 649–664.

Porter, L. W., & McKibbin, L. E. (1988). Management education and development: Drift or thrust into the 21st Century. New York: McGraw-Hill.

The Economist, (2011). Trouble in the Middle: Is time running out for business schools that aren't quite elite? *The Economist.* October 5.

Trapnell, J. E. (2007). AACSB International accreditation: The value proposition and a look to the future. *Journal of Management Development, 26*(1), 67–72.

Urgel, J. (2007). EQUIS accreditation: value and benefits for international business schools. *Journal of Management Development, 26*(1), 73–83.

Chapter 1

The Current State of the Business School Industry

Introduction

This chapter summarises the current literature related to business schools and their evolution. It also introduces a value chain framework for considering the various activities within business schools. This is then used to anchor a review of business school offerings in Chapters 2 and 3. Chapter 1 concludes with a consideration of potential innovations in business models in management education based on comparison with other industries.

The literature concerning business schools and their component activities and parts is extensive; to do justice to this overall body of writing is not the goal of this overview. (However, for a thorough review see Hommel and Thomas (2014).) Instead, it seeks to provide a typology of the type of writing that exists to highlight the ongoing challenges, issues and themes in the field.

It is important to note here that in most cases business schools are actually quite small businesses. This exacerbates the complicated nature of myriad value chains. While there are of course exceptions, most business schools, in our experience, generate an annual turnover in the tens, not hundreds, of millions of dollars or euros. They often have a faculty base of 50 to 100 academics and generally a similar number of additional service and professional staff.

With such a relatively small base, running multiple business lines within a business school is quite challenging with many of them under-resourced and under-scaled. So, how did we get to this place: a complex model with vastly different offerings under one roof and apparently carrying a torch for higher education?

What are the history and critical perspectives on business schools and their evolution?

Business School Histories

There are many business schools and they all regularly have anniversaries, at which point many commission a book to capture the history of their school (Barsoux, 2000; Broehl, 1999; Copeland, 1958; Cornwall-Jones, 1985; Cruikshank, 1987; Gitlow, 1995; Sass, 1982; Sedlak & Williamson, 1983; Van Metre, 1954). This vein of literature is interesting historically and it is quite enjoyable to look at the pictures to see whom one knew or knows. However, the vast majority of these books cover "the great men" who were instrumental in moving a particular school forward and who often were wearing marvellous suits and sometimes had odd sideburns. But it is not easy to identify any individual book that seriously tries to deconstruct the value creation processes of an individual school.

Association Histories

A second set of books broadens out from a narrow focus on an individual institution to provide an overview of the business school landscape. These books tend to be the product of business school associations. The two-part AACSB *History* with the first volume covering the era from 1916 to 1966 and the second from 1966 to 2006 (AACSB, 1966 and Flesher, 2007 respectively) reviews the evolution of the association, of accreditation, of governance and globalisation, and of thought leadership and advocacy.

The EFMD volume *Training the Fire Brigade: Preparing for the Unimaginable*, published in 1996, reflects through the insights of well-regarded European management development professionals on the origins, roots and evolution and future pathways for the organisation. It also explores the European education model.

There is also a series of books written on behalf of national associations. For example, Williams (2010) catalogues the 60-year history of UK business schools from the perspective of the UK's Chartered Association of Business Schools. Brailsford (2012) edits a series of viewpoints on the content and challenges of business education in the Asia-pacific region from the perspective of AAPBS, the Association of Asia-Pacific Business Schools.

While there is a sensible measure of self-reflection, these types of books are again mostly commissioned works celebrating anniversaries and milestones rather than works of critical analysis.

Critical Overviews Prior to the Advent of Rankings

Though there are a few critical overviews of business schools, Khurana (2007), a renowned Harvard business school professor, outlines the history and evolution of American business schools from their beginning in the late 19th and early 20th century. He shows how business schools evolved from, effectively, vocational trade schools through to their present state. He cites the tremendous influence that the Ford and Carnegie Foundation Studies of 1959 had in the repositioning of business schools from practical institutions into academic behemoths. But he also notes that management education at that time could, and perhaps should, have professionalised itself with a code of conduct and an ethical anchor. Instead, the drive to an academic status and the "marketisation" of education within business schools turned them into advocates for shareholder value and profit maximisation rather than educational guardians setting out to create responsible professionals as do other professional schools such as engineering, law or medicine.

The two studies mentioned above, known as the Foundation Studies, are central to an understanding of business education and the business of business schools for every dean and senior business school manager around the world even if the circumstances for their emergence and influence originated outside the US. The studies are named after two large philanthropic foundations in the US that emerged from the vast fortunes generated by the first wave of US industrialisation in the late 19th and early 20 centuries. The two foundations were the Carnegie Foundation and the Ford Foundation. As Khurana outlines, foundations, between 1900 and 1935, provided 64% of all grants to US universities both for new initiatives and for existing institutions.

After the Second World War, financial support was concentrated on existing institutions and very quickly linked to business schools. Both the Carnegie and Ford Foundations felt that the poor quality of business schools threatened not only the actual schools but, more importantly, in the midst of the Cold War threatened the health of the economy, democracy and the American way of life in the face of communism. Throughout the 1950s, while the Carnegie Foundation wrote reports and made grants to ensure that a significant element of liberal arts education was present in undergraduate courses, Ford concentrated its efforts on graduate schools of business and focused its "big push" on "centres of excellence", first at Harvard, Columbia and Carnegie Tech (now Carnegie-Mellon University) subsequently at Chicago and Stanford, and latterly trickled down to important schools at UCLA,

Berkeley and MIT. By 1960 $35 million had been donated, which is at least $200 million in today's money. And with that much money at stake, there were strings attached.

Schools were to professionalise with faculty holding doctorates and producing graduate-level academic publications; students were to be taught quantitative methods and behavioural sciences — and only those academically qualified were to be admitted. And, while not obviously stated but clearly understood, schools were to have an anti-communist, pro-business and clearly capitalist orientation.

While the grants that flowed in the 1950s set the scene, the 1959 Foundation Studies codified the expectations and created the framework for the dominant business school model and paradigm (see Thomas, Lee, Thomas, & Wilson, 2014), which still, for better or worse, exists today. It has undoubtedly played a key role in setting the expectations for faculty activities and has consequently set the parameters for the financial structure of most business schools.

The 1959 Carnegie report was written by Swarthmore College economist Frank C Pierson and led to the general studies requirements in US undergraduate business degrees. More recently, the Colby report (2011), sponsored again by the Carnegie Foundation and the Aspen Institute, expressed concern that the liberal tradition in undergraduate business programmes is being undermined by a curriculum that has become too technical and narrow.

The more profoundly game-shifting Ford Foundation report was written by Robert Gordon and James Howell, both of whom had been involved directly in Ford Foundation activities but also held academic positions at Berkeley and then Yale and then Stanford. The conditions that were attached to the grants made to the centres of excellence effectively became the rules of the game for all business schools seeking to compete with them.

In 1988, following the three decades of the "golden age of business schools" (Augier & March, 2011), Porter and McKibbin wrote their report *Management Education and Development: Drift or Trust into the 21ˢᵗ Century*. At this point the validity of the dominant model was being questioned. In their introduction, the authors clearly stated that their broad study, in essence framed as a thoughtful critical review, was the first of its kind since the Carnegie and Ford reports of 1959. Indeed, Porter and McKibbin were commissioned to write up the various AACSB seminars and workshops delineating the then-present and likely future state of business education. These studies, collectively known as the Futures Studies, also included a European perspective facilitated by EFMD.

The authors supplemented the workshops with a more formal study, surveying business school deans and faculty as well as employers and other interested parties. Visits were made to 10% of the then 600-plus AACSB-accredited schools. The study also looked at executive education for the first time.

The book examined systematically what the Foundation Studies had found in 1959 and updated each element of the business school portfolio to discuss the changes that had taken place since that time. It is organised basically as an AACSB accreditation visit with chapters covering the curriculum, students and graduates, faculty, teaching, research and scholarship, university and business community relations, and then four long chapters on executive education. It should be noted, however, that while international input was sought, the actual output of the book primarily focused on the US business school environment.

Porter and McKibbin, effectively marked the end of the of the golden age of business schools and is the tombstone of the pre-rankings era – there is not a mention of rankings because there were none at that point.

Khurana (2007) in his book quotes extensively from an interview with Andy Policano (2005), an influential US business academic, and it is worth repeating the quote here:

> "Few people can remember what it was like before 1987 – what I call the year before the storm. It was a time when business school deans could actually focus on improving the quality of their schools' educational offerings. Discussions about strategic marketing were confined mostly to the marketing curriculum. PR firms were hired by businesses, not business schools. Most business schools had sufficient facilities, but few buildings had marble floors, soaring atriums, or plush carpeting. Public university tuition was affordable for most students, and even top MBA programs were accessible to students with high potential but low GMAT scores. (p. 340)"

The "storm" of rankings changed everything. In the simple terms of this literature overview, the 25 to 30-year hiatus between the Foundation Studies and the Future Studies, was succeeded by a "storm" of literature about business schools. In the "grand scheme of business schools", rankings, for better or worse, marked the dawn of the era of business schools as businesses.

Critical Overviews and Major Studies Since the Advent of the Rankings Era

Thomas, Lorange and Sheth in their 2013 overview *The Business School in the Twenty-First Century* provide a social constructionist theoretical model (see Table 1.1) of business school evolution that delineates the institutional and international development of business schools across five generations of business school evolution (see Tables 1.1 and 1.2). Here we start with the "trade school" and "golden age" generations (following from the Ford and Carnegie reports) that precede the era of rankings in the late 1980s. The era of rankings, while hotly contested, became a source of business school legitimacy and the basis for the intense competition in today's environment.

They also provide an excellent update on the period since the introduction of rankings. Indeed, one can clearly see the different emphasis and orientation unleashed. Whereas prior research efforts concerned themselves with the quality of a business school *per se*, this and a kinder and gentler era disappeared once rankings had been introduced. Pettigrew, Cornuel, and Hommel (2014) stress the importance of the international comparative perspective and method in understanding the evolution of business schools and it is worth repeating the quote here:

> "In their recent book, *The Business School in the Twenty-first Century*, Thomas, Lorange, and Sheth (2013) offer the most comprehensive account yet of the rise and rise of the business school and the challenges of delivering management education in the contemporary world. Their analysis of evolution of business schools, and their search for identity and legitimacy, places these issues in the context of the modern university and society. They also provide the most international account yet of the variety of business school forms, identities and models throughout the world. Using a social constructionist theoretical approach, they point to the diversity of types of business school within and between the nations and regions, as well as the standardizing influences in those same locations from the impact of accreditations and ranking systems. Their

Table 1.1. Social Constructionist Model of Business School Evolution.

Generation and Time Period	Behavioural Characteristics and Causes	Implications and Consequences	Legitimacy Providers
First generation (19th century to early 20th century) Emergence of alternative business school models 'Trade school' Vocational era	Different knowledge structures, frames of reference and cognitive maps Different beliefs about management education but mainly vocational trade-type models focusing on commercial and administrative practice	Beliefs about market boundaries vary across countries Differential rates of growth and adoption across countries Influence of culture, regulations, country characteristics, and languages evident at local and national level Size of schools tends to be nationally determined	• The creation of managerial employment by industrialists, entrepreneurial individuals and the state to cope with larger organisations • Institutionalised managerial systems (e.g. accounting practices) • Establishment of AACSB (1916) and subsequent accreditation systems for business schools
Second generation (early 20th century to 1970s) Clearly shaped national schools	Strategic reference points established in countries – the United States model is key reference point Imitative behaviour at a local/national level	The identification of national role models and a dominant industry recipe means that differences exist among the key drivers of:	• National governments • Universities • 'Feeder' disciplines (economics, psychology)

Table 1.1. (*Continued*)

Generation and Time Period	Behavioural Characteristics and Causes	Implications and Consequences	Legitimacy Providers
	The image and identity of a business school becomes clear Institutionalising processes	• Governance • Funding and endowment • International mindset • Innovation • Knowledge transmission • Corporate linkages	
Third generation (1970s–1990s) Dominance of US business school model Growing strength of national champions	Industry recipe is established – dominant design/role model is evident Reputational structures and clear identities formed Internationalising processes Organisational adaptation and interpretation Benchmarking processes	Issues of image and reputation become important Social capital is built up long term Rankings and league tables become indicators of success International alliances form to enhance reputations of leading schools in the US and Europe	• Research rankings and citations • Globalised performance measures and rankings • National performance measures • International accreditation bodies (e.g. AACSB, EFMD AMBA)

Fourth generation (1990–2005) Strong emergence of European business school model			
Mounting criticism of US business school model	Recipe includes:	The Bologna Accord in higher education (common degree structures and credit transfer)	
European industry recipe is established (mimicry of US model challenged)	• Largely one-year MBA model	Role of EFMD	
Emphasis on internationalisation and public management	• Strong executive education focus	• Founding of EQUIS accreditation system as European accreditation	
Clear European identity sought (EU etc.)	1. Push for softer skills and innovation linkages to the role of business and government in society	• High rankings for European schools (HEC, IESE, INSEAD, LBS) in FT rankings	
Executive education and corporate relevance/linkages important	2. Competing on high-quality research as per US model but strong focus on impactful research		
Strong decline of state funding of higher education in general and management education in particular	• INSEAD opens campus in Singapore – slogan 'The Business School for the World'. Other schools follow international expansion approach		
Strong reputations/identities developed for European schools	• EFMD launches CEIBS as a business school in Shanghai in partnership with City of Shanghai		
INSEAD			
IMD			
LBS etc.			
Little private/endowment funding			

Table 1.1. (Continued)

Generation and Time Period	Behavioural Characteristics and Causes	Implications and Consequences	Legitimacy Providers
Fifth generation (2005 to present) Strong range of global models Globalisation in emerging markets (Asia, Eastern Europe, Latin America)	Shift of global economy from West to East. Increasing criticism and blame attached to business schools for the global financial crisis (e.g., teaching ambassadors of market capitalism) Issues of ethics, corporate social responsibility and sustainability become central to business schools Questioning of market capitalism – search for a broader stakeholder view of management Influence of governments in Asia on business school development very strong (e.g., Singapore, Hong Kong, China)	Adaption of the business school models to different cultures, political and economic systems Clear strategic reference points (business schools) emerge CEIBS (Shanghai) FUDAN (China) HKUST (Hong Kong) NUS (Singapore) Getulio Vargas (Brazil) IIM (India) ISB (India) IEDC (Slovenia) Skolkovo (Moscow) Continued questioning of the role and purpose of business schools • Is it a professional school? • Alternative models?	CEEMAN develops accreditation for schools in Eastern Europe Increasing number of business school associations: • CLADEA (Latin America) • AAPBS (Asia Pacific) • AIMS (India) Role of EABIS (Europe), PRME/GLRI (EFMD), UN Global Compact and Aspen Institute in promoting ethical/societal values Strong ranking of Asian schools (CEIBS, HKUST and ISB) in FT rankings

| Generation 5b Globalisation in emerging markets | Africa rising: promise of strong economic growth
• VUCA environment
• Traditions of communitarianism, family focused webs of obligations
• Issues of ethics, CSR in governance
• Role of public / private sectors in management education | Adaption of business school models to African traditions/linguistic/cultural differences
• Weak business school ecosystem
• Huge demand for management education
• A few (8–10 elite schools; e.g., GIBS, UCT, WITS, Stellenbosch, Strathmore, Lagos, GIMPA)
• 100 or so business schools
• Alternative models/executive education, massification low cost | • AABS collaboration network and local accreditation
• Some influence of international accreditation agencies (AMBA, EQUIS, AACSB) but few accredited
• One or two schools (e.g., GIBS in FT rankings)
• Emerging entrepreneurship network |

Source: Derived from Thomas et al. (2013, p. 18)
Note. Sourced from *Africa: The management education challenge* (pp. 108–111), by Thomas, Lee, Thomas, & Wilson, 2016, Bingley, UK: Emerald Group Publishing Limited.

Table 1.2. Differences between Business Schools in Regions of the World.

		Europe	The United States	Asia	Africa
Institutional differences	Language/ culture/ regulation	Many languages; 27 nation states (EU) Multi-cultural Heavy regulation	Single language More homogeneous culture Low level of regulation	Many languages Mix of mature and newly emerging countries Multi-cultural Heavy government involvement (e.g. China, Singapore)	Many languages 54 nation states Multi-cultural Many tribal cultures (micro-trending) Increasing public school regulation
	Standardisation	Slower acceptance and institutionalisation of business schools	Fast acceptance and institutionalisation of business schools	Rapid growth of business schools since 2000	Relatively slow growth of business school – about 100
	Size	Small to medium size (c. 250 business schools)	Medium to large size (c. 800 business schools)	Generally small size (but growing number)	Public sector funded schools large; private sector small

Competitive differences				
Governance/values	Predominantly public funding Strong public-sector linkages	Predominantly private funding Weak public-sector linkages (state governments)	Strong public funding	Primarily public funding Increasing private sector investor
Funding and endowment	Small endowments Weaker resource base	Large endowments Strong resource base	Some endowment funding Resource base strong in mature economies	Weak resource base Virtually no endowment
International mindset	International in outlook Students/faculty more international	International in outlook Students/faculty more international	Regionally focused Mix of local and foreign faculty (50/50)	Tend to be country / regional focused Mainly African students Some international partners in top tier schools
Innovation	Practical, problem-based learning Critical reflective thinking Range of models: one-year MBA,	Two-year model for MBA Discipline- and research-based	Range of models but generally one-year Asian case development	Mix of US / European models with local adaption Some online / blended learning.

Table 1.2. (*Continued*)

	Europe	The United States	Asia	Africa
	distance learning, action-oriented learning		Mix of US and local models	Attempts to leverage mobile technology
Knowledge transmission/ corporate links	Knowledge conveyed in books and practice-oriented journals; Greater reliance on executive education; Closer to business	Knowledge conveyed in discipline- and research-based journals; Fewer schools promote executive education	Focus on A-journals, peer review and publications; Relevance to business and corporate linkages important; Executive education growing	Practical / vocational relevance; Executive education important for upskilling; Practically oriented research
Social capital differences — Rankings	Lower overall rankings in league tables; Favoured for international	Higher overall rankings in league tables; Favoured for initial salary,	Six Asian schools in FT rankings; Strong on research	Hardly any schools in FT rankings; Largely African rankings (e.g., Financial Mail)

	outlook, career progress, value for money	salary progress, alumni and research quality	quality, student quality
Reputation	Some strong brands but generally lower brand identity and reputation	Many strong brands – particularly private schools. High brand identity and reputation	A few strong brands but social/ reputational capital growing	A few strong schools in South Africa, Egypt, Ghana, Kenya, Nigeria, North Africa (about 10 in total) Social / reputational capital growing slowly

Source: Derived from Thomas et al. (2013, p.18)
Note. Sourced from *Africa: The management education challenge* (pp. 112–113), by Thomas et al., 2016, Bingley: Emerald Group Publishing Limited.

analysis of the possibilities of business school diversity, in amongst more conventional accounts of the homogenization, is a welcome relief and keeps open the debate about the extent of convergence and divergence in the business school development. However, their treatment of that debate is ultimately limited by their reliance on secondary sources to map and explain the parameters of similarity and difference. This continuing empirical deficiency, in what is an otherwise comprehensive illuminating account, points again to the need for comparative international research to map and measure similarity and variation in the development of business schools" (p. 298).

Of the authored books, as opposed to edited collections that grew rapidly during this period, titles emerged such as *The Collapse of the American Management Mystique* (Locke, 1996); Crainer and Dearlove's *Gravy Training: Inside the World's Top Business Schools* (1999); *The Business School and the Bottom Line* (Starkey & Tiratsoo, 2007); *From Higher Aims to Hired Hands: The Social Transformation of American Business Schools and the Unfulfilled Promise of Management as a Profession* (Khurana, 2007).

These books often contained justified criticisms of business schools and their managerialism while other books published recently have generally been more benign and have looked at more specific areas. The clear exceptions are two books, sponsored primarily by EFMD (following its 40th anniversary) (Thomas et al., 2014; Thomas, Thomas, & Wilson, 2013), which, through extensive interviewing, not only examined and catalogued the many criticisms of business schools but also sought to critique meaningful pathways for the growth of the field.

Other writers have tried to focus on particularly important issues on the change/future agenda. For example, Iniguez de Onzono (2011) seeks to create a better bridge between academia and *agora* — between gown and town — to help transfer, through the twin pillars of teaching and research, more learning into society. Iniguez's 2016 book *Cosmopolitan Managers* continues this trend (Iniguez de Onzono, 2016). He is interested, as the subtitle notes, in executive development that works. Fraguiero and Thomas (2011) focus on the strategic leadership processes in practice and try to explain the "what", "why" and "how" of the links between context, processes and outcomes. They model business schools as professional service firms and use that framework to examine the strategic process of internationalisation, evolution and competition between IMD, INSEAD and London Business School (LBS) over the period 1990-2004. Schoemaker (2008) details the implications of future challenges to business schools, stressing teaching, research and institutional development.

In terms of the teaching paradigm, business schools need to shift to a more real-world approach and problem-centric style, bringing in industry speakers, encouraging team work among students as well as giving students an opportunity to be co-creators of the educational content and learning experience.

As institutions they need to rethink the costs and benefits of tenure, to try and recreate a better academic career path, look at scholarship from a broader point of view and encourage alliances beyond their ivory towers while still maintaining their core values.

Business schools need to view themselves more as a set of stakeholder relationships than a physical place of learning. Pettigrew et al. (2014) note that such rich processual treatment is an important research area in understanding the international dynamics of business schools.

In 2011, AACSB published its work on the *Globalization of Management Education*, which, as its subtitle emphasises, looks at *Changing International Structures, Adaptive Strategies and the Impact on Institutions*. It concludes that globalisation, internationalisation and trade radically change the content of management education in terms of contextual, cultural and global intelligence (AACSB International, 2011). Two previously mentioned empirical studies, Thomas et al. (2013, 2014) focus on the current challenges and future pathways. The first volume – *Promises Fulfilled and Unfulfilled in Management Education* (Thomas et al. (2013) delineated the successes and the many criticisms and crises facing management education (see Box 1.1).

The second in 2014 – *Securing the Future of Management Education: Competitive Destruction or Constructive Innovation* - outlines the many challenges hindering the future development of management education. Collectively they point out a series of "blind spots" in the field (see Box 1.2). These perceptual gaps may have resulted from individual human factors or institutional pressures (such as rankings or professional accreditations) that serve to homogenise the perspectives and frameworks of business school deans or university presidents and lead to imitative behaviour and shared external norms.

Such behavioural norms are often described as "dominant logics" – shared views in the management education field that result from the collective experience and common mental models of senior business school and university administrators (Prahalad & Bettis, 1986). An example of

Box 1.1. Issues and Criticisms

The significant criticisms of business schools include the following (Thomas et al., 2013, pp. 66−68):

- The business school lacks identity and legitimacy in the modern university and society in general (Wilson & Thomas, 2012)
- The business school is a socialisation mechanism (Grey, 2005) − a business school is a necessary rite of passage for senior management and more a "finishing school" than an intellectual, liberal-thinking cauldron of activity
- The business school overemphasises shareholder capitalism and does not embrace the models of stakeholder capitalism (Locke & Spender, 2011; Muff et al., 2013)
- The business school does not provide a clear sense of purpose, morality and ethics with respect to its role in society (Colby, Ehrlich, Sullivan, & Dolle, 2011; Ghoshal, 2005; Millar & Poole, 2011)
- The business school focuses on analytics/ scientific rigour at the expense of developing wisdom, interpersonal and leadership/ management skills (Bennis & O'Toole, 2005; Mintzberg, 2004; Schoemaker, 2008)
- The business school produces self-referential research that is seen as irrelevant (Hambrick, 1994; Pfeffer & Fong, 2002, 2004)
- The business school embraces scientific rigour at the expense of other forms of knowledge (Schoemaker, 2008; Thomas & Wilson, 2011)
- The business school has pandered to business school rankings and has become too responsive to the consumer voice (Khurana, 2007)

In addition, Dean Canals the recently outgoing dean of the IESE Business School (2011) more recently offered a series of observations on the purposes of business school. He identified a series of crises (Thomas et al., 2013, pp. 15−16):

- The business school's role in the ethical and moral crisis of scandals such as ENRON and the financial crisis
- The need to take globalisation seriously
- The relationships between the dean and the university and the dean and the faculty
- The sustainability of business models and funding sources

- The perception of the increasing irrelevance of business school research
- The search for stakeholder capitalism and the definition of senior managers' roles and responsibilities in society.

Note: Sourced from *Promises Fulfilled and Unfulfilled in Management Education* (pp. 15−16; 66−68), by Thomas, Thomas et al., 2013, Emerald. Bingley, UK: Copyright Emerald Group Publishing Limited. Reprinted with permission.

Box 1.2. "Blind spots" and Critical Issues

- The impact of technology
- The relevance gap between academia and practice
- The paradigm trap in business school curricula
- The ethics, CSR and sustainability debates
- The importance of entrepreneurship
- The discussion of social and management innovation and business model innovation
- The lessons of leadership
- The localisation versus globalisation rhetoric in the field.

Note: Sourced from *Securing the future of management education: Competitive Destruction or Constructive Innovation?* (pp. 153−154), by Thomas et al., 2014, Bingley, UK: Emerald. Copyright by Emerald Group Publishing Limited. Reprinted with permission.

---

a "dominant logic" is the role of the MBA as a general management degree. Despite criticism (such as Mintzberg, 2004), it has proved a "killer" product in management education over many years and is still highly valued by business school deans. Many students regard it as an essential rite of passage if they aspire to reach the C-suite of their organisations.

More importantly, the crowdsourcing, business education "jam" carried out by business school scholars from the Questrom School at Boston University in the US points to the need for more innovation in business education and its models, advocating an open innovation approach (Carlile, Davidson, Freeman, Thomas, & Venkatraman, 2016).

Finally, Thomas et al. (2016) have also spent considerable effort in mapping the business school landscapes in emerging markets such as Africa and subsequently in Latin America. They conclude that business school models and curricula need to be sensitively adapted to the contextual and cultural requirements of each emerging market region.

There is also a plethora of edited volumes on business schools. In general, they are compilations arising from academic conferences, business school anniversaries or taskforces often promoted by professional associations or entities in the business school eco-system.

They tend to provide largely benevolent, occasionally pointed, views of various elements of business school life. *New Challenges for the Business Schools* (van Baalen, 1995), for example, has chapters on the benefits of interdisciplinary education and the search for rigorous and relevant research. *Disrupt or be Disrupted: A Blueprint for Change in Management Education* from GMAC in 2013 is quite an interesting volume from the perspective of this book as it does look *inter alia* at the business of business schools in some chapters.

Pettigrew et al. (2014) book on the institutional development of business schools, based on an EFMD/HERC research conference, usefully summarises existing research and suggests three important research themes: comparative research on the international development of business schools; comparative research on performance differences in business schools; and micro-level studies of the processes, practices and performance of business school faculty in different academic areas and regions of the world.

Muff et al. (2013) in *Management Education for the World*, writing on behalf of the GLRI (Global Leadership Responsibility Initiative), develop a curriculum that addresses the need for radical change in the relationship between business schools and the various stakeholders in society. This is endorsed by Morsing and Rovera (2011) in pointing out the need for business schools to examine more closely the issue of how to secure a sustainable future for an increasingly global society.

Other authors have focused on executive education and more practical topics. Canals, in 2015, edited *Shaping Entrepreneurial Mindsets: Innovation and Entrepreneurship in Leadership Development* (Canals, 2015). In a similar vein, but specific to executive education, the 5th edition in 2010 of a series of handbooks published by Gower looked at overall learning strategies and specifically at learning interventions (Gold, Thorpe, & Mumford, 2010). Hind, in 2015, does something similar with *Management Development that Works* (Hind, 2015).

Journal Articles and Recent Focus on Management Education

If books have proliferated since the dawn of the rankings era, articles have appeared like water from a fire hose. The 2002 launch of the Academy of Management's journal *Learning and Education* marked the significance of studies about business education. It has featured much-cited and often controversial articles about the short-comings of business education. For example, Jeffrey Pfeffer and Christina Fong wrote "The End of Business Schools? Less Success than Meets the Eye" in 2002. Henry Mintzberg and Jonathan Gosling, also in 2002, wrote "Educating Managers beyond Borders" (Mintzberg & Gosling, 2002). And the late Sumantra Ghoshal published "Bad Management Theories are Destroying Good Management Practices" in 2005.

Bennis and O'Toole contributed "How Business Schools Lost their Way" to the *Harvard Business Review* in 2005. Ken Starkey and various co-authors also regularly critique management education in the business school setting. Antunes and Thomas (2007) explored the competitive advantages and disadvantages of European business schools. What has always been of some surprise with each of these articles and criticisms is that they are coming from within the system and from people who have done quite well from the system. But that is another matter for another day.

Yet all of them, as well as the critical overviews and edited books, have challenged the lack of change and model innovation in business schools, noting the clear evidence of a dominant paradigm centred on the Gordon/Howell Ford Foundation prescriptions of the 1960s. How then can business schools' business models be adapted to take account of not only the environmental context but also the role of business and management in a responsible and sustainable way?

Value Chain as a Mapping Approach

As an organising principle in considering the management of the business school and the associated activities and offerings consider a simple value chain as in Figure 1.1. Of course, not every school is active across the whole spectrum of programme possibilities and not all value chains will therefore carry the same relevance. Depending on the unique situation of each institution, the value chain will be re-configured to reflect the business system and processes of each level of a business school's offerings and activities

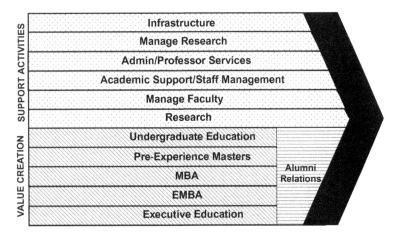

Figure 1.1.   Business School Value Chain.

At each level, beginning with undergraduate education and proceeding along a probably arbitrary age-influenced continuum, there are different components that comprise that chain, drivers that are relevant, and the skills and competencies a school requires at that level. Also important to examine are the increasing elements of disruption and substitution that have come to play a significant role.

Schools increasingly face "make or buy" decisions at practically each stage of the value chain. At one end of the spectrum there are schools where almost everything is managed and delivered in-house. At the other end, there are schools that function largely as co-ordinating mechanisms for the purchasing of external services. At nearly every stage of the continuum there are now complementary service providers who will come to the aid of schools to help them provide needed capabilities. These services do not come cheap nor minus attached strings. If this book achieves one thing it will be to encourage business schools to think through the consequences, short-term and long-term, of their own structures and financial arrangements.

Getting it wrong, allowing external providers to cherry-pick lucrative services and price them to their own advantage rather than to the advantage of a school is something we have seen increasingly over the past decade. Whether we like it or not, business schools need to be managed in a business-like, professional and careful manner whether they are long-established incumbents or new-comers to business education or to one of the distinct value chains in the mix of programme possibilities.

Business Model Considerations

Recent interest in business models and business model innovation has sparked new research into the business model construct as well as the potential for disruption in various industries, not least in the business school industry.

Zott and Amit (2010) define a business model as a "system of interdependent activities that transcends the focal firm and spans its boundaries" (p. 217). The rise in research and perspectives on business models has led to a new focus on this concept as a holistic approach for value creation (Amit & Zott, 2001).

Indeed, the attention on business models has caught the attention of scholars as evidenced by the thousands of articles published in both academic and non-academic journals.

One of the central roles of a business model is that of innovating the traditional application of processes, technology and organisational constructs of a firm. Chesbrough (2003) suggested that open innovation beyond the boundaries of the firm would definitely lead to the identification of new sources of value. While the active work of scholars has furthered our understanding and application of the business model concept, few business school scholars have looked in the mirror to evaluate or refresh the business model of the business school.

One such effort to rethink the fundamentals of the business school was sponsored by the Boston University Questrom School of Business in 2014. The business education "jam", an open-invitation approach designed in association with the Watson division of IBM, provided over 6,000 participants with the aim of understanding the challenges and opportunities that may lead to future innovation in the way we frame business school education. In a summary of this business education jam, the organisers note: "Our business model for education, rooted in an outdated model, is unsuited for student-centred mastery of learning and thinking. In other words, we offer standard products and services while students demand tailored solutions (Carlile et al., 2016).

Several new trials and reviews of various management education models have started to reshape the management education landscape (Thomas, Lorange et al., 2013). Examples include the blended learning model, which reduces the need for physical assets, as well as the practice-oriented model that focuses on postgraduate and executive education with a "relevance" orientation. Some of these models are illustrated in Figure 1.2 and are summarised along with other potential models in the following section.

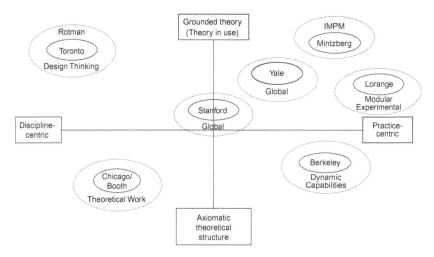

Figure 1.2.   Business Model Types.

Mintzberg IMPM (International Master's Program in Practising Management) model – This model uses design principles of interactive, integrated learning and learning from experience from cross-disciplinary perspectives to understand and develop the process of managing. It treats management as a practical role and links education to practice. Based on five modular themes (Managing oneself, Managing relationships, Managing organisations, Managing context and Managing change), the modules focus on operational excellence and value creation.

HAAS/ Berkley Dynamic Capabilities Model – This aims to build innovative business leaders by moving from an implicit to an explicit culture, from a co-ordinated to capabilities-integrated curriculum, from an independent experimental learning programme to an integrated experimental learning curriculum. The model aims to provide foundations from which leaders who emerge with all the necessary skills that a manager must have to redefine the art of management.

Rotman design thinking model – This offers the so-called 3D MBA, which is deep, broad and dynamic and based on design thinking. It works on the development of holistic, creative and critical thinkers. These thinkers are expected to make decisions that are moral and ethical following the ideals of a "liberal arts" MBA. Students are exposed to a broad spectrum of models that address the complex and messy nature of business problems.

Stanford, Yale and the Jain/Stopford Programme for a global curriculum — These schools attempt to address the challenges of globalisation. Yale breaks out of the mould of elite MBAs and offers programmes that address different organisational perspectives, including that of investors and customers in a global context. Stanford emphasises multidisciplinary traditions through its programmes that address global contexts. The aim of the model is to produce managers who think critically and analytically about complex problems that they must solve and make decisions with compassion and an ethical compass.

Open University blended learning model — For many years, the Open University in the UK has developed a pioneering platform for blended learning using a practice-based model, which thrives on the creation of student-based learning and networking communities. While web resources and previously television programmes did the teaching, a key element of this model is the presence of synchronous networking components. The programme is built around a high-quality and innovative curriculum.

Focused innovation model (UC San Diego) — This school offers an MBA focused on innovation. The first year of the MBA programme has a 12-month, three-course sequence that is conducted parallel to the basic MBA courses. The first includes ideation (idea generation), research and development and prototyping. The second and third semesters break students up into teams to develop an idea, come up with a business plan and receive guidance from venture capitalists, faculty and practitioners. The MBA tries to integrate technology with management skills and offers problem solving through the application of several sources of knowledge, including a design thinking orientation.

The GLRI 50 + 20 project — The project offers a new stakeholder management perspective focused on societal needs such as sustainability. It aims to ensure that business, management and leadership schools provide relevant and holistic education and research. They look to enhance student leadership skills focused on responsible, ethical and sustainable decision making and critical thinking and reasoning.

Starkey's knowledge model — This offers a knowledge perspective using a four-fold strategy — knowledge for management, knowledge for society, knowledge about management and knowledge about society.

Network model (Lorange) — This is based on the former Lorange Institute in Zurich (now known as CEIBS, Europe), which focuses on a practical executive MBA and executive education short courses. It offers many modules over the weekends so that it is easy for participants to work as well. The modules are offered jointly for executives and master's students with faculty recruited from all over the world, usually practitioners with unique backgrounds and expertise.

Alternative Possible Business Model Approaches

While the migration to new forms of management education provision will continue to grow and evolve, it is worth considering a range of business models that have already caused disruption in other industries and may do the same in management education. These ideas are not predictions but rather proposed as deliberate provocations to an industry that seems ready for disruption if unready to address the many challenges it faces. While these ideas may seem far-fetched and capable of being casually dismissed, there is an element of reality in considering the potential for disruption that may come from outside our industry.

Freemium business model — This offers basic services at no cost and charges a premium for additional services. Examples of this include Linkedin, the popular business-networking site (which now includes Lynda, a business education component) along with Skype, the internet-based communication firm. Could management education be provided in a Freemium model? What if basic management courses were available free (perhaps as basic MOOCs with some form of certification) and more advanced courses were offered at a premium?

Disintermediation business model — This sells directly without the traditional middlemen or aggregator. Could management education be provided by instructors without the involvement of a business school? Of course, only institutions can grant degrees but what is the incremental value of the degree over the knowledge? As we have already seen with the Khan Academy, a pioneer in online/blended learning that focuses on teaching the basic concepts of every subject, educators can be successful in providing education without an institution.

Network orchestrator model — This model pairs the customer and the buyer by creating a network of peers to sell products/services, build relationships and collaborate. Examples of this include eBay, Uber, Alibaba and Tripadvisor. Could a network of management development educators be formed that transcends the traditional institutional boundaries? What if an aggregate executive education course catalogue was created complete with ratings, comments and suggestions?

Razor/blade model — This offers product below cost to increase the volume of lower-margin sales. Examples include computer printer firms that lock consumers into the purchase of their unique ink cartridges or the eponymous razor blade holder dependent on expensive blades. The reverse model can also work such as the case of the iPod with iTunes. Could an MBA degree be coupled with ongoing executive education sessions to lock-in managers?

Subscription business model — In this model, customers are charged a subscription fee to obtain access to the service. While this is an old model, Netflix disrupted the home movie market with this simple concept. Could management education be provided as a subscription service?

Fractionalisation business model — This sells the partial use of something that may not be achievable directly. The sharing economy is booming and is affecting many industries. Examples are time-share vacation condos and NetJets private air service. Could a seat in an EMBA programme be shared between groups of colleagues who could otherwise not experience an executive level of master's education?

Product to service model — Instead of selling the product, this model sells the service that the product performs. Examples include Zipcar, Citi Bike and GE Aircraft Engines. These allow customers to use the product without the hassles of ownership. In the case of management education, could this translate to more of a "management consulting" project-based model where students bring problems and we draw on the disciplines of business to help solve them?

Crowdsourcing model — This model seeks to facilitate a large group of people to contribute (for no compensation) in exchange for access to the collective contribution. Examples of this include YouTube and Wikipedia, where many people make contributions. While this is somewhat akin to academic research publishing, the management education content and experience is generally closely guarded by the provider. Could a crowdsourcing model of management education provide a different service to those seeking to further their management knowledge?

User community model — This provides membership that allows access to a network while capturing membership fees and advertising. An example of this is Angie's List, a site that helps consumers evaluate home improvement providers. Could a user community model be a future way of engaging alumni?

Long-tail model — Rather than requiring high volumes, this model creates specialised products that appeal to unique groups. Lego is a great example of changing its product types to the building of specialised kits that appeal to niche customers. In business schools we are already seeing the shift from high-volume MBA programmes to more specialised master's programmes that fit with given professions (finance, communications, HR).

While there are probably many more potential ideas and considerations for the future business model of the business school it must be recognised that such models need adaptation. Each business school has a unique market, geography, context, culture, positioning and set of competencies that must be taken into account in forming an appropriate design.

Summary and Conclusions

This chapter has listed the criticisms and blind spots evident in the management education system as noted by many writers and critics. In particular, it has noted that as educators often write about the importance of business model innovation and talk increasingly at conferences about the need for innovations yet often cling to a dominant design and MBA-led paradigm. The different business models that already exist today are often minor variants of the dominant paradigm of education. A thorough understanding of value chains and platform models will help build frameworks that deepen the understanding of disaggregation and disintermediation (Chapters 2 and 3), leading to increased innovation. While there are many potential ways that our industry might see disruption in the future, there is an increasing sense that, one way or the other, the current model of business education will change.

References

AACSB. (1966). *The American Association of Collegiate Schools of Business, 1916-1966*. Homewood: R.D. Irwin.

AACSB International. (2011). *Globalization of management education: Changing international structures, adaptive strategies, and the impact on institutions (Report of the AACSB International Globalization of Management Education Task Force)*. Bingley, UK: Emerald Group Publishing Limited.

Amit, R., & Zott, C. (2001). Value creation in e-business. *Strategic Management Journal, 22*(6-7), 493–520.

Antunes, D., & Thomas, H. (2007). The competitive (dis)advantages of European business schools. *Long Range Planning, Elsevier, 40*, 382–404.

Augier, M., & March, J. G. (2011). *The roots, rituals and rhetorics of change: North American business schools after Second World War*. Stanford, CA: Stanford University Press.

Barsoux, J. (2000). *INSEAD: From intuition to institution*. London: Palgrave Macmillan.

Bennis, W., & O'Toole, J. (May 2005). How business schools lost their way. *Harvard Business Review, 83*(5), 96–104, 154.

Brailsford, T. (2012). *Business education in the Asia-Pacific: Contexts and challenges*. St. Lucia, Queensland: University of Queensland Press.

Broehl, W. (1999). *Tuck and Tucker: The origin of the graduate business school*. Hanover: University Press of New England.

Canals, J. (2015). *Shaping entrepreneurial mindsets: Innovation and entrepreneurship in leadership development*. IESE Business Collection. Hampshire: Palgrave Macmillian.

Carlile, P. R., Davidson, S. H., Freeman, K. W., Thomas, H., & Venkatraman, N. (2016). *Reimagining business education: Insights and actions from the business education jam*. Bingley, UK: Emerald Group Publishing Limited.

Chesbrough, H. W. (2003). *Open innovation: The new imperative for creating and profiting from technology*. Boston, MA: Harvard Business School Press.

Colby, A., Ehrlich, T., Sullivan, W. M., & Dolle, J. R. (2011). *Rethinking undergraduate business education: Liberal learning for the profession*. John Wiley & Sons.

Copeland, M. (1958). *And mark an era: The story of Harvard Business School*. Boston: Little, Brown and Co.

Cornwall-Jones, A. T. (1985). *Education for leadership: The international administrative staff colleges 1948-84*. London: Routledge and Kegan Paul.

Crainer, S., & Dearlove, D. (1999). *GravyTraining: Inside the business of business schools*. San Franciso: Jossey-Bass.

Cruikshank, J. (1987). *A delicate experiment: The Harvard Business School 1908-1945*. Boston, MA: Harvard Business School Press.

Flesher, D. (2007). *The History of AACSB International Vol. 2 1966-2006*. AACSB.

Fragueiro, F., & Thomas, H. (2011). *Strategic leadership in the business school: Keeping one step ahead*. Cambridge: Cambridge University Press.

Ghoshal, S. (2005). Bad management theories are destroying good management practices. *Academy of Management Learning & Education, 4*(1), 75–91.

Gitlow, A. (1995). *New York University's Stern School of Business: A centennial retrospective*. New York: New York University Press.

Gold, J., Thorpe, R., & Mumford, A. (2010). *Gower handbook of leadership and management development* (5th ed.). Farnham, Surrey: Gower.

Grey, C. (2005). *A very short fairly interesting and reasonably cheap book about studying organizations*. London: Sage.

Hambrick, D. (1994). What if the academy actually mattered? *Academy of Management Review, 19*(1), 11–16.

Hind, P. (2015). *Management development that works*. Faringdon, Oxfordshire: Libri Publishing.

Hommel, U., & Thomas, H. (2014). Research on business schools: Themes, conjectures and future directions. In A. Pettigrew, E. Cornuel, & U. Hommel (Eds.), *The institutional development of business schools* (pp. 6–35). Oxford: Oxford University Press.

Iniguez de Onzono, S. (2011). *The learning curve: How business schools are re-inventing education.* Spain: IE Business Publishing.

Iniguez de Onzono, S. (2016). *Cosmopolitan managers: Executive development that works.* London: Palgrave Macmillan.

Khurana, R. (2007). *From higher aims to hired hands: The social transformation of American business schools and the unfulfilled promise of management as a profession.* Princeton, NJ: Princeton University Press.

Locke, R. R. (1996). *The collapse of the American management mystique.* Oxford: Oxford University Press.

Locke, R. R., & Spender, J. C. (2011). *Confronting managerialism: How the business elite and their schools threw our lives out of balance.* London: Zed Books Ltd.

Millar, C., & Poole, E. (2011). Ethical leading in a global world – a roadmap to the book. In C. Millar & E. Poole (Eds.), *Ethical leadership: Global challenges and perspectives.* Basingstroke, UK: Palgrave Macmillan UK.

Mintzberg, H. (2004). *Managers, not MBAs: A hard look at the soft practice of managing and management development.* London: Pearson Education.

Mintzberg, H., & Gosling, J. R. (September 2002). Educating managers beyond borders. *Academy of Management Learning & Education, 1*(1), 64−76.

Morsing, M., & Rovira, A. S. (2011). *Business schools and their contribution to society.* Los Angeles: Sage Publications.

Muff, K., Dyllick, T., Drewell, M., North, J., Shrivastava, P., & Haertle, J. (2013). *Management education for the world: A vision for business schools serving people and the planet.* Edward Elgar Publishing.

Pettigrew, A. M., Cornuel, E., & Hommel, U. (Eds.). (2014). *The institutional development of business schools.* Oxford: Oxford University Press.

Pfeffer, J., & Fong, C. T. (2002). The end of business schools? Less success than meets the eye. *Academy of Management Learning & Education, 1*(1), 78−95.

Pfeffer, J., & Fong, C. T. (2004). The business school 'business': Some lessons from the US experience. *Journal of Management Studies, 41*(8), 1501−1520.

Policano, A. (2005). What price rankings? *Biz Ed*, an AACSB publication, September-October.

Prahalad, C. K., & Bettis, R. A., (1986). The dominant logic: A new linkage between diversity and performance. *Strategic Management Journal, 7*(6), 485–501.

Sass, S. (1982). *The pragmatic imagination: A history of Warton School 1881-1981.* Philadelphia: University of Pennsylvania Press.

Schoemaker, P. J. H. (Spring 2008). The future challenges of business: Rethinking management education and research. *California Management Review, 50*(3).

Sedlak, M., & Williamson, H. (1983). *The evolution of management education: A history of the Northwestern University J. L. Kellogg Graduate School of Management 1908-1983.* Urbana, Chicago: University of Illinois Press.

Starkey, K., & Tiratsoo, N. (2007). *The business school and the bottom line.* Cambridge, UK: Cambridge University Press.

Thomas, H., Lee, M., Thomas, L., & Wilson, A. (2014). *Securing the future of management education: Competitive destruction or constructive innovation?* (Vol. 2). Bingley, UK: Emerald Group Publishing Limited.

Thomas, H., Lee, M., Thomas, L., & Wilson, A. (2016). Africa: The management education challenge (Vol. 1). Bingley, UK: Emerald Group Publishing Limited.

Thomas, H., Lorange, P., & Sheth, J. (2013). *The business school in the twenty-first century: Emergent challenges and new business models.* Cambridge, UK: Cambridge University Press.

Thomas, H., Thomas, L., & Wilson, A. (2013). *Promises fulfilled and unfulfilled in management education* (Vol. 1). Bingley, UK: Emerald Group Publishing Limited.

Thomas, H., & Wilson, A. D. (2011). 'Physics envy', cognitive legitimacy or practical relevance: Dilemmas in the evolution of management research in the UK. *British Journal of Management, 22*(3), 443−456.

Van Baalen, P. J. (1995). *New challenges for the business schools.* Erasmus University: Eburon Publishers.

Van Metre, T. (1954). *History of Graduate School of Business, Columbia University.* New York: Columbia University Press.

Williams, A. P. O. (2010). *The history of UK business and management education.* Bingley, UK: Emerald Group Publishing Limited.

Wilson, D. C., & Thomas, H. (2012). The legitimacy of the business of business schools: What's the future? *Journal of Management Development, 341*(4), 368−376.

Zott, C., & Amit, R. (2010). Business model design: An activity system perspective. *Long Range Planning, Elsevier, 43*(2-3), 216−226.

Chapter 2

Undergraduate and Pre-Experience Programmes

Introduction

Not all business schools, including some of the more elite names, offer undergraduate degrees in business studies. But those that do provide different approaches and designs. Colby, Ehrlich, Sullivan, and Dolle (2011) provide an extensive review of mainly American models of four-year provision with a strong focus on general studies. In contrast, European programmes tend to be more specialised, typically lasting three years with a fourth-year pre-experience master's taken in addition. Yet there are many alternative models available within the US and Europe as well as a range of approaches in emerging markets.

This chapter explores the value chains of the various components and activities involved in handling undergraduate and pre-experience programmes in greater detail.

Undergraduate Management Education

It is quite difficult to run a school without students—however much business school professionals sometimes think it would be quite pleasant. Jesting aside, finding students differs tremendously according to national location and the current reputation of a particular school. The value chain for undergraduate education is shown in Figure 2.1.

Find Students

At a base level, there are generally national application systems in place. In the UK, for example, UCAS (the Universities and Colleges Admissions Service) allows candidates to select a defined number of universities that they would like to attend. This includes all university courses including management education. If they achieve the grades necessary

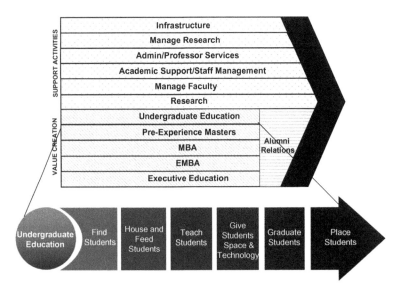

Figure 2.1.   Undergraduate Education Value Chain.

to gain admittance, they will receive an offer to attend. The university's/ school's role then becomes one of yield management to ensure that an ideal number of students attend. Too few and there will be a negative effect on income; too many and they may have trouble coping.

Prior to 2015, government student quotas were in place for universities in the UK. If surpassed these could have a detrimental effect on a university's funding allocation across faculties or to the overall quota for the Institution. At present, the system is becoming more competitive across the overall higher education system and quota caps have been removed so that competition is fiercer than ever.

A second round of direct applications take place over the summer with a "clearing" process that is effectively a matching service between would-be students who have not been offered a university place and universities with spare slots on programmes. Predictions for 2018 were that 25% of students would come through clearing either as a second chance or, increasingly, as direct applicants who have not applied through UCAS (Education UK, n.d.).

Comparable national systems exist in most other countries. In some cases, they are, like UCAS, driven effectively as a matching service. In others, admissions are driven by results through national exams where all students compete for the highest grades and universities/schools pick off the best possible students possible, depending on their own rankings and prestige.

At this primary level of recruitment, the role of a business school is to generate the highest possible level of awareness and prestige among graduating secondary school students (and their parents). The benefit is that one knows where the potential students are – they are still at secondary/high school. Marketing aimed at them occurs through direct interaction with targeted students, open days on campus or through outreach by the targeted schools.

An undergraduate business degree has been the most popular university programme since 1981 and the number of students opting for a business degree has been increasing (Desilver, 2014). The business schools targeted by secondary students (and their parents) are often carefully chosen – either for academic quality or the ability of the students/parents to pay the business school's tuition.

Marketing also entails an entire "student happiness" industry of guidebooks covering everything from the quality of the education through to local pubs and the price of beer and food. Most business schools are aware of these drivers in student recruitment, as they are effectively the most traditional and representative avenues for attracting students.

The Use of Agents

National, post-secondary school recruitment is a core part of recruitment but it is not the only, nor necessarily the most important, at least not in financial terms. Vast numbers of international students are not directly recruited but are found via agents – especially across Asia and in certain parts of Africa. They are often charged school fees substantially higher than the tuition charged to domestic or near-domestic students.

A survey conducted by Observatory on Borderless Higher Education (OBHE) in late 2012, provides several insights from the 181 higher-education institutions across seven countries surveyed. These institutions were degree-granting universities and colleges.

The highlights include:

- The majority of higher education institutes engage education agents
- The majority of the agent relationships reported came mainly from Asian markets (Hong Kong, Japan, South Korea, Thailand, Vietnam) as well as Brazil, Nigeria, Saudi Arabia and the UAE
- China recorded the highest number of agents used

Table 2.1.   Percentage of Students Recruited Through Agents for Selected Sestination Markets.

Country of Recruiting Institution	Proportion of International Students Recruited through Agents (Average Percentage)
Malaysia	56
Australia	53
New Zealand	47
Canada	41
UK	38
Netherlands	20
United States	11
OVERALL	38

Note: Adapted from *The agent question: insights from students, universities and agents.* Observatory on Borderless Higher Education, Retrieved from http://www.obhe.ac.uk/. (OBHE, 2014).

- There were large variations when it came to the distribution of international students recruited via agents as shown in Table 2.1. However, the average recorded was approximately 33% across all markets while it was 38% among the seven top destination markets.
- Institutions across the board expressed satisfaction with their relationships with agents. Reasons included "great market coverage", delivery of "better-prepared and counselled students", local knowledge and cultural sensitivity, and promotion of institutional brands.
- Dissatisfaction with the agent relationships came from agents taking "maximum share with minimum risk", generating greater administrative workload and individually producing a low influx of business. They also failed to meet expected conversion rates, demonstrated a lack of consistency in expertise across markets and did not meet contracted targets.
- Australia and New Zealand had the longest history of contracting agents and rely the most on agents as a means of recruitment while Malaysia has more recently attracted international students through an agent network.
- The most common compensation method to agents are commissions, ranging from a minimum of 10% to 17.4% of first-year tuition as shown in Table 2.2.

Table 2.2. Average Agent Commission Rates for Selected Destination Markets.

Country of Recruiting Institution	Minimum % (Average)	Maximum % (Average)
Australia	11.5	17.4
Canada	11.5	15.0
New Zealand	10.0	15.0
UK	10.4	15.8
United States	10.0	12.3
All Sectors in Sample	10.7	15.1

Note: Adapted from *The agent question: insights from students, universities and agents.* Observatory on Borderless Higher Education, Retrieved from http://www.obhe.ac.uk/. (OBHE, 2014).

- Formal agent contracts were prevalent across all seven countries. A majority of the institutions judged the renewal of contracts through performance management and reviews. However, in the US only a quarter of the institutions cited this practice, which is perhaps an indication that such relationships are less developed and formalised in the US.

The OBHE examined a subset of international business school data covering 48 comprehensive universities in Australia, the UK and the United States, representing about 27,000 first-year international students. The highlights include:

- 32% of the students in the sample had engaged an education agent, an increase of 10% compared to five years ago.
- The youngest students, such as those searching for admission to undergraduate programmes, are much more inclined than more mature students (searching for entry to doctorate studies) to use agents
- The likelihood of using agents was greater in key Asian markets as shown in Figure 2.2.
- There was a higher likelihood of international students in Australian schools having engaged an agent (50%) in comparison to British or American schools (27%). The report states that "the higher Australia ratio is consistent with near-universal use of agents among the

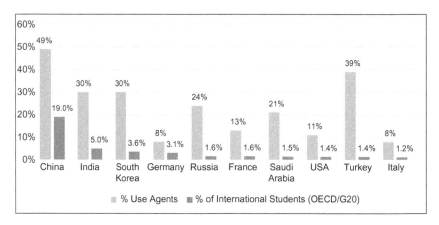

Figure 2.2. Agent Usage for Selected Countries. *Note*: Adapted from *The agent question: insights from students, universities and agents.* Observatory on Borderless Higher Education, Retrieved from http://www.obhe.ac.uk/. (OBHE, 2014).

nation's universities, and Australia's longer-established and more active regulation of agents".

- Students did not find agent certification or an institute's endorsement of an agent significant in their search for agents. The best method to attract students to engage agents was through the competence of an agent to market and make their services known
- Agents were of comparable influence to institutional websites in the aspect of enrolment decisions among surveyed students. (32% vs 37% respectively — a noted difference compared to 2007, where the results were 12% vs 44%)
- The use of agents was more prevalent for students who enrol at lower-ranked universities compared to the more prestigious ones as shown in Figure 2.3. The report suggests that this finding may be due to the more complicated and risky process of understanding lesser-known choices.
- There is a broad variation in how much students compensate agents, from nothing (25%) to more than US$5,000 (13%), with an average estimated at US$500.
- Among the students who engaged agents, a great majority reported being "satisfied" regardless of the compensation amount with some feeling "very satisfied". In fact, even among students paying an agent in excess of US$5,000, 75% felt satisfied or better.

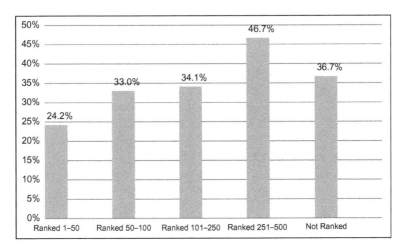

Figure 2.3. Reported Use of Agents by First-year International Students, by Ranking in the Academic Ranking of World Universities. *Note*: Adapted from *The agent question: insights from students, universities and agents.* Observatory on Borderless Higher Education, Retrieved from http://www.obhe.ac.uk/. (OBHE, 2014).

In looking at the some of the volumes in the OBHE tables, it is apparent that agent management is a core requirement for universities in general and business schools in particular – especially as most agencies are in fact quite small and often employ under five agents altogether.

Somewhere along the line, a new group of organisations arose: effectively agents-plus or "super-agents". They noted that the recruitment fee of on average $500 for a student was considerably less than the programme tuition charged to those students. Any market disparity attracts new entrants and in this case, the newcomers created a more wide-ranging recruitment process, which straddled language teaching and university admissions. In some cases, the service provision extends even to student housing.

Companies like StudyGroup and INTO in the UK and Navitas in Australia have scaled-up to develop an internal, employed agents network alongside a pattern of relationships with agents who remain independent. Navitas says that it has 120 recruitment staff in 20 offices managing over 4,000 recruitment partners in over 130 different countries (Navitas, n.d.). They provide services to just less than 30 universities in the large, student-importing English-language markets of

Australia, Canada, New Zealand, the UK and the US (Chartered Association of Business Schools, 2016).

In aggregate, they claim to provide a range of educational services to over 80,000 students through more than 120 institutions. Given that not all potential international students speak sufficient English, these super-agents also design and deliver pathway programmes either as a foundation year or as an extended first year of studies using university premises or in several cases build additional university premises to teach and support their students (ICEF Monitor, 2014).

INTO, for example, notes that its partnership model covers recruitment and English-language provision but also includes the creation of "desirable living spaces". Its website promotes the idea of a recruitment/language-training/accommodation partnership with universities. This began in 2006 with an agreement between INTO and the UK's University of East Anglia, resulting in a 35-year joint venture partnership (INTO, n.d.).

This is not the place to either judge or evaluate the contractual benefits or otherwise of an agreement between a university and its business school and an external provider. However, any contract with a commercial organisation that extends for 35 years is surely a gift that keeps on giving, for better or worse, and that will impact generations of deans and business school managers to come. The clear concern is about whether someone thought it through well enough to insert some renegotiation points, or break clauses, into the agreement.

House and Feed Students

Student housing, beyond the combined provision with recruitment companies, has become an enormous business unto itself with similar issues of concern. For example, private providers own approximately 45% of the 330,000 beds at universities in the UK (UK Council for International Student Affairs, 2016). The range of types of ownership is broad. In Nottingham, 79% of beds are privately owned while in large university towns such as Oxford and Cambridge, the number is closer to 10% (GVA, 2013). Two companies, UNITE and University Partnership Programmes (UPP), control 35% of all of the private provision in the UK (Unite Group, n.d.; University Partnerships Programme, n.d.).

Early in 2016, the issue of student housing flared up at University College London (UCL), one of the most prestigious UK universities. In this particular case, students went on a rent strike to protest at both the basic levels of rent and regular rent increases. While housing at UCL is owned by the university, the onward march of private provision is unlikely to be halted (Kollewe, 2016).

In looking at the housing component element of the value chain, there are, of course, a wide range of perspectives that are relevant. Business schools are not really in the business of student housing but obviously students need accommodation. Students are also traditionally a challenge to house. There are myriad issues of health and safety, life-styles and general liveliness to deal with but probably most important is that students only really want accommodation for the part of the year in which they are studying. Charging for 12 months when only eight are used annoys students. Scaling the rent for each of the eight months to cover 12 is seen as very expensive accommodation.

From that perspective, outsourcing of non-core school services has many advantages including risk sharing and limited capital allocation. On the other hand, in extrapolating from the challenges faced by UCL, one can see that there are also potential downsides such as fixed con-tracts and limited flexibility. Ensuring good management and sensible pricing for years into the future from an outsourcing partner requires skills that are not necessarily available in every business school.

Teach Students

Now that our conceptual business school has collected up sufficient stu-dents and found them a place to stay, it is time to deliver the education the students have come to acquire. Traditional faculty members, fully employed by universities and business schools, have a range of activities that they are expected to perform. While the actual combination of teaching, researching and service changes significantly depending on the nature of the particular institution and the characteristics of the individual faculty member, there is a range that is not uncommon.

Business schools that strive to achieve, or maintain, accreditation status need to focus on ensuring that faculty members are sufficiently academically active. Even within these institutions, there is a significant range of expectations. That said, the four categories of faculty classifica-tions – scholarly academic, practice academic, scholarly practitioner, instructional practitioner – used by AACSB can help provide some insight.

Scholarly academics are expected to produce refereed articles in recognised academic publications in their own fields and tend to focus more on research than teaching; they will be expected to teach in a range from 90 to 200 hours a year. *Practice academics* are expected to publish but not to focus on academic refereed journal articles and will teach 150 to 250 hours per year. *Scholarly practitioners* focus on teaching but do develop pedagogic material including new courses and material as well as contributing articles and case studies for use in the classroom and will be expected to teach in the range of 250 to 300 hours. *Instructional practitioners*, often non-academics who are experts in their fields – accountants would be a typical example, will teach 350-plus hours per year because they focus on teaching and are not involved in the traditional academic, publishing and research life of the school.

Data released from the 2014/15 Higher Education and Student Affairs (HESA) Staff Record provides some details with regard to staff employment at UK higher education providers (HEPs). On 1 December 2014, the number of staff employed in the HE sector totalled 403,835, excluding atypical staff – reflecting a 2% increase from the 395,780 staff employed the year before. Of these, 49% (198,335) were employed on academic contracts in 2014/15, the same percentage reported in 2013/14 (HESA, 2016). The bulk of these were in professional occupations. Figure 2.4 presents the number of staff by contract type and mode of employment.

There were 272,250 staff employed on full-time contracts, an increase from 263,050 in 2013/14, and 131,585 employed on part-time contracts, which decreased 1% from 132,730 in 2013/14. Over the 2014/15 academic year, the number of atypical staff employed by HEPs on academic contracts numbered 75,560, a 1% increase from 2013/14.

There were 31, 345 atypical staff reported on non-academic contracts in the 2014/15 return. HEPs are only required to return atypical staff on academic contracts and thus the number of atypical staff on non-academic contracts may be higher than reported.

The traditional faculty model described above, however, is an illusion for all but the best-financed institutions. The financial structures and consequences of faculty composition are dealt with later in the book but suffice it to say here that having faculty who concentrate on research and spend a proportionally small amount of time on teaching costs money. Research is not cheap!

What is evident, and again this does not apply to all schools, is that a binary structure has developed under the radar in many business

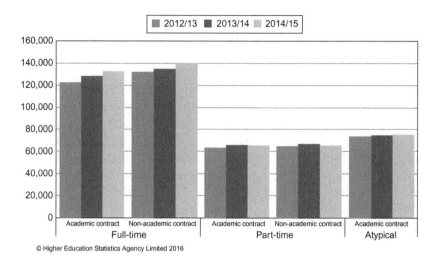

© Higher Education Statistics Agency Limited 2016

Figure 2.4. Staff at HE Providers by Mode of Employment and Academic Contract Market 2012/13 to 2014/15. *Note: Adapted from Staff at higher education providers in the United Kingdom 2014/15* by HESA Higher Education and Student Affairs. Retrieved from https://www.hesa.ac.uk/news/21-01-2016/sfr225-staff. (HESA, 2016).

schools. The "proper" faculty members are referred to as institutional resources while a reserve army of labour, contracted on an annual or spot-market basis (so-called zero hours contracts), provide vast amounts of the teaching. In the UK, as the HESA data shows, half of the staff involved in academic activities overall in the university sector were on part-time contracts (HESA, 2016).

Without looking at the faculty composition and specific teaching load allocations on a school-by-school basis, it is impossible to generalise for all schools. However, it is easy to imagine fingers waving in the air around the world in business schools that state they ensure that only fully employed, all-round, research-active faculty teach on their programmes. For some schools, this may well be the case.

For other institutions, however, there will be many instances where a significant proportion, if not all, of a programme is taught by adjunct faculty. In terms of undergraduate programmes there is, of course, a certain logic that adjuncts, or at a minimum teaching-heavy faculty, are involved at this stage. Many undergraduate programmes courses are of an introductory rather than advanced level – and thus having faculty who specialise in teaching and who are often a variable resource can be considered academically appropriate and financially sensible.

Faculty composition is also affected by where a programme is delivered. Students studying on the home campus will often have a different experience than students studying on satellite campuses, whether they are regional metropolitan centres or further afield. This gets exacerbated when programmes are taught at even greater distances in other countries – often in emerging markets. At the ultimate extreme, there are entire business schools that are effectively without a permanent home faculty and use only adjuncts. In fact, there is a UK-based professional services outsourcing company that supplies all the faculty for the London operations of three different business schools.

There are no value judgments to be made on the models used for faculty and the relative proportion of research versus teaching faculty or between permanent, structural faculty and adjuncts with longer or shorter-term contracts. There are strengths and weaknesses to all models and thoughtful business school management simply needs to be cognisant of the trade-offs involved.

As noted earlier in this examination of undergraduate education – at one end of the spectrum there are business schools that manage student recruitment and housing themselves and have a full-service faculty, active in research and education. At the other end of the spectrum, there are schools that have effectively outsourced all of the above. Most institutions lie somewhere between. Across the overall spectrum, there is a need, as this book maintains, to reflect on the actual business of business schools, on how we tackle these issues today, to assess how we expect the landscape to evolve in the coming years and to conjecture what effects this will have on our own institutions.

Provide Space and Technology

The traditional model of a business school is an institution with functionally fit-for-purpose buildings on a campus or in stand-alone facilities that are maintained by the university and including catering and maintenance departments. Business schools that have the means – through reserves, fundraising or long-term loans – seek to invest extensively in their facilities in order to impress potential students – and their parents. One of our colleagues described his experience in a school in New England in the US as presiding over a country club in which students sought not only state of the art business school buildings but ever-larger sports and recreation facilities, and concert and event venues.

This traditional model, however, is not the reality for many business schools that are unable to generate sufficient funding for such capital-intensive projects. The previous section discussed the possibility of working with service providers such as Navitas, StudyGroup, INTO, UPP and UNITE for student accommodation. These organisations are, of course, also in a position to provide teaching and learning space for students, extending the infrastructure that they presently provide for introductory and foundation year courses.

An alternative to building one's own facilities or working within a building and infrastructure partnership is to simply rent buildings. In London, a host of business schools from outside the city have leased buildings in order to bring their schools to where students wish to be rather than fight the difficult fight of getting students to come to campuses that are not necessarily top travel destinations nor centres of commerce and thus areas of potential post-study employment. At the undergraduate level, satellite facilities or leased primary facilities at least have a semblance of campus life since the vast majority of students study on a full time basis. In the sections below on postgraduate study, we will revisit the subject of facilities for those types of programmes.

As with physical space, virtual space can also be provided in any number of ways. In some cases, business schools have built online learning platforms from scratch (although this has receded in recent years) and in others business schools have worked with "learning management system" (LMS) providers such as Moodle, Blackboard and Canvas to source their basic infrastructure, which is then filled with course material and other content from resident faculty.

What has been interesting to observe over the past five years or so has been the online emergence of provision from for-profit sources. This has first been through the experience gained by previously fully for-profit providers of online education. The second has been from companies specifically set up to provide "white label" [unbranded] provision, effectively turnkey provision of online learning for traditional business schools. A key driver here is that established schools can charge significantly more for their degrees than can online providers who do not have a strong market reputation.

An example of a for-profit online provider is Embanet. After Pearson paid $650 million to buy Embanet Compass in 2013, several senior leaders left the company. Pearson, an established UK education company with about $7 billion in revenue, is incorporating parts of the Embanet unit with its eCollege business to serve the changing college landscape and appeal to an increasing number of online students (Rivard, 2013).

Embanet, like Bisk, Deltak, Academic Partnerships, 2U and other "enablers", assists colleges in shifting for-credit courses from the classroom to the web. In the process, these companies are able to receive about 50% of tuition revenue from students, which results in the enabling business being potentially profitable. It is presently unclear whether the personnel changes at Embanet will affect Pearson's client pool; at the time of the acquisition, Embanet had 35 university clients while Pearson had 10.

As noted in the article quoted from *InsideHigherEd*, a number of managers from Embanet left the company after the Pearson acquisition. Besides former Embanet CEO Steve Fireng, Pearson also lost at least three others who had joined the company as part of the Embanet deal. The former executive vice-president of business development, chief financial officer and chief operating officer all left either to competitor companies or to explore new opportunities.

Many others went to Keypath, which provides similar services. In the UK, an arm of the Open University called Future Learn can also provide online learning in a box.

What to do about online learning is a decision every business school must make for itself. Indeed, all approaches involve a significant amount of investment − financially and academically − the costs just come at different points. Creating a course internally involves a significant investment in terms of setting up the course in the first place and an ongoing effort in student recruitment for all of the subsequent years, though the income does go back directly to the school.

Working with a white label provider incurs smaller, sometimes zero, up-front costs but inevitably will lead to a revenue-sharing or a profit-sharing arrangement of some sort for many years. Calculating whether a white label provision is a positive financial arrangement is a big challenge. Sharing revenue is all well and good but it is invariably the business school that carries the costs for the bulk of the education. And business schools are not great at calculating the costs of providing education − as a subsequent chapter in this book will illustrate in greater detail.

Profit sharing is even more fraught. Coming to an agreement on which costs should be allocated to various activities within a school almost always leads to fierce arguments about which programme or activity should carry which proportion of the library, gardeners or other facilities. Extending costing model discussions from the business school to an external for-profit partner can lead to real tears. Over the past number of years, colleagues have told stories at annual conferences about deals that sounded great initially but turned into nightmare arrangements when the for-profit partners pointed to the fine print in long-term contracts.

A business school need not own all its own resources but contracting with external partners requires serious thought, good advice and significant legal support, ideally with break clauses in contracts to either renegotiate arrangements or to exit altogether.

Graduate and Place Students

While students, hopefully in nearly all cases, seek to learn during their studies, they definitely want to graduate and to receive confirmation that they have graduated by receiving their degree. In many cases, principally in the US, degrees can only be conferred by business schools that have received the right to award degrees through the state in which the school is registered. Generally, this is completed together with approval from one of the seven regional accrediting bodies in six US regions. However, in other more diverse geographies other arrangements are possible and common.

In the UK, achieving "degree awarding powers" (DAP) is a long and involved process for business schools and other HEIs that were not automatically granted DAP through their status as traditional universities. At present, there are only about a dozen HEIs that have been granted DAP outside of the historical group. That said, there are a whole host of specialised, or newer, institutions that provide undergraduate as well as postgraduate education and seek to provide credentialing to their students. They can do so through validation services. These services require the validating provider to ensure that the educational provision at the partner institution is of sufficient quality and on a par with the quality of the education at the providing institution and in line with the requirements of authorities such as the Quality Assurance Agency in the UK, which oversees, and regularly reviews, the quality of higher education in the UK.

Such validating services are not only possible within the UK but are extended to institutions around the world in no small number. According to Education UK, which promotes UK higher education, 590,000 students around the world receive UK degrees without actually attending a UK-based university. It is hard to ascertain how many of these degrees are specifically in business education rather than in other subjects but given that business education accounts for about 15% of overall studies, the number is significant (Education UK, n.d.).

According to Education UK, some highlighted benefits of studying for a UK qualification overseas are: reputation and quality, cost, career and flexibility. There were several options in how to obtain a UK qualification overseas − distance or online learning, international branch campuses, franchised programmes, twinning, validation, joint, double or dual degrees, credit transfer, top-up programmes, and full-time or part-time study.

For distance learning programmes, classes can be conducted on various platforms such as online via forums, instant messaging, social media, blogs and email. Some have "virtual" lectures and seminars with students participating via webcams. Course materials can be sent in print or on a CD. These courses are optimal for part-time study but students are required to be disciplined in completing all assignments and projects on time.

An increasing number of universities are allowing students the opportunity to take some of their courses as a Massive Open Online Course (MOOCs). There is no fee required to participate in MOOCs though a fee is required for a certificate at the end of the course. The number of universities offering students the choice to convert MOOCs into degree credits is increasing. Several universities offer scholarships to students who do very well in a MOOC.

A number of UK universities have international branch campuses in other countries. These campuses often reflect the UK atmosphere whereby lessons are taught in English and some faculty members and students come from the UK. Franchised programmes are sometimes called $3+0$ programmes − a UK degree course studied completely at a local institute. A licence is given to the local institution to teach the course. However, the UK institution manages academic standards and awards the final certification (Commission on Institutions of Higher Education (CIHE), n.d.).

Twinning programmes are joint-study programmes, where students get to study at both the local and overseas university at specified stages. These programmes are available as $2+1$, $1+2$, $1.5+1.5$, the former number indicating the number of years spent studying locally, the latter overseas study. Joint-study programmes are popular with US universities to provide international experiences for students without creating an adverse impact on the timeline for graduation.

Joint, double or dual degree programmes are collectively developed and recognised by two or more institutions. There may be home country staff teaching in the local institution and some courses involve a year abroad. At the end of study, students either receive independent degrees from the two institutions or a joint one from both — the former being dual awarded the latter a joint award.

Credit transfer, also known as "articulation" or "study abroad" involves a university recognising the credits obtained from studying at a local institute. Some students may begin their studies locally and continue abroad, transferring all credits obtained.

Postgraduate Pre-experience Master's Education

After examining the value chain in undergraduate business education the focus now turns to post-graduate pre-experience education with an emphasis on the differences rather than processes that are similar. The value chain is shown in Figure 2.5.

Find Students

Attaining a viable class of pre-experience master's students is a different and brisker challenge than finding students for undergraduate education

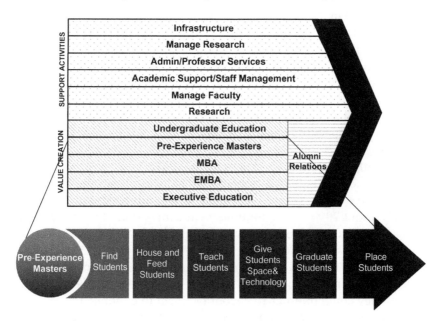

Figure 2.5.   Pre-Experience Master's Value Chain.

as described earlier. The challenge of where to find the majority of pre-experience candidates is not all that difficult – given that they are largely pre-experience, the likelihood is that they are already at a university completing their undergraduate education.

From here, however, paths to recruitment diverge considerably depending on where a school is located.

In 1999 Europe saw the introduction of the "Bologna Accord", which sought to harmonise the disparate European higher education systems into a three-stage progress of bachelor's, master's and doctoral education. While this sounded like non-news to many business schools in the English-speaking world, it was a radical change for most of the national systems on the European Continent, where higher education, specifically business education, was based on a two-stage process of an extended first degree: *Diplom Kaufmann* in Germany, *Doctorandus* in the Netherlands, *Magister* in Austria and so on followed by doctoral-level education as the second stage.

In a study by the Graduate Management Admissions Council (GMAC) (instigated and co-chaired by one of the authors of this book), it was estimated that the potential new market size for master's programme candidates, students who previously would have graduated with a Master's degree but would henceforth be "bachelor's graduates" was around 2.4 million students a year.

At one end of the spectrum, it was expected that students from countries where the previous system was a combined bachelor's/master's would graduate from a bachelor's degree, register directly for a master's degree and not attend the master's programme if they had found a suitable job. Given that employers had the choice of many students who continued to study and to complete their master's degree, the uptake of direct employment after a bachelor's degree only reached about 20%.

At the other, more Anglo-American, end of the spectrum and based largely on the UK and Irish markets, it was clear that about 80% of bachelor's graduates seek employment after undergraduate education and only about 20% would continue – at some point – to study at the graduate level (U.S. Department of Education, National Center for Education Statistics, 2016).

The market that developed rapidly involved Continental business schools attempting to hold on to as many of their own bachelor's graduates as they could in order to encourage them to continue their studies at their home school. A second effect was to attempt to attract graduating students from slightly less prestigious schools in one's home market — stealing the cream of the crop from the local competition as it were. A third effect was the realisation that restricting oneself to one's home market and offering master's degrees only in indigenous languages hugely restricted the potential recruitment of international students, especially in "small language" countries. Thus, the vast majority of business master's programmes offered across Europe are now offered in English.

As an aside, some anomalies to the system described above have always existed. France historically had a split system that required students to attend a *Class Preperatoire*, effectively years one and two of study, before they attended any of the *Grandes Ecoles*. A further effect triggered by Bologna but which has taken more time to develop and establish itself properly in some European markets has been the upgrading of Technical Schools from a historical "lower level" positioning something akin to a bachelor's, to a recognised bachelor's within the Bologna progression and another feeder to pre-experience master's degrees. For the historical combined bachelor's and master's schools as well as for schools that originated in an Anglo-American system additional student recruitment takes place by reaching more directly into the market for students through the usual channels of direct marketing, student recruitment fairs, agents and other forms of global recruitment. In the UK, for example, non-UK students at master's level in universities overall account for over 200,000 students. At business schools, non-EU students alone account for nearly 60,000 students. Counting in EU but non-UK students adds further large numbers.

Thus, in Europe, at a minimum, the "action" within the business school market is taking place primarily at the pre-experience, often specialised, master's market. New programmes continue to be designed and marketed. Thoughtful schools realise that this market is large and will continue to be large for many years to come. They also realise that while tuition revenue is often not as high as for MBA programmes, the cost of sales is also not as high as for the MBA.

In other markets, primarily in North America, the size and scale of the European pre-experience market is often met with incomprehension and confusion. This is, of course, understandable given the historical education system of bachelor's and master's that exists in those markets. Even so, there is real potential for schools in the US and Canada to tap into an enormous international market of pre-experience students who, rather than wait to gain an MBA, would cherish a master's degree and graduating from a North American school.

House and Feed Students

Much of the detail of student accommodation and hospitality services was covered in the earlier section on undergraduate education. Here, there are a couple of key differences. Certainly in the UK, most pre-experience post-graduate business students are international and thus look to a business school to offer them accommodation. Given that most pre-experience post-graduate courses last for one or two rather than three or four years, student accommodation requirements are easier for schools to provide and can often be charged out at higher rates than undergraduate accommodation. The second difference is that as students progress from undergraduate through postgraduate education, their expectations of the quality of the overall buildings and facilities increase.

Many universities may not provide housing for graduate students, who must find available housing through university agents. Many schools promote this as "independent living", positioning it as a step towards an independent lifestyle following university studies. In fact, this approach allows the school to avoid the heavy capital expenses associated with housing.

Teach Students

We noted earlier that to ensure sufficient provision and accessibility for international students, many post graduate pre-experience programmes are taught in English rather than in the native language of a business schools not located in an English-speaking country. This can provide quite a challenge in staffing terms for an institution.

Teaching successfully in one's native language is already testing; teaching in a second language is even more daunting. Second, given that the student population is often significantly internationalised, students will seek out international faculty to teach them and provide cases and examples that speak to an international cohort of students. Thus it is evident that there is increasing pressure on faculty that becomes initially significant at the postgraduate level and especially so in executive education.

Over the years there have been all kinds of models on how business schools should organise the transition between undergraduate and post-graduate education. In some cases, there are separate undergraduate and postgraduate schools within the same university, effectively autonomous of each other. In other cases, where the school is integrated, a sort of apartheid exists between those who teach undergraduate students in the local language and those, including resident international faculty, who can or can only teach in English. Where the local supply of English-language faculty is insufficient, visiting, adjunct faculty are called upon to teach. This can involve a few visitors to add additional colour and experience or it can lead to a situation where most of the faculty, in some cases all of the faculty, teaching on postgraduate courses are virtual rather than permanent. This trend is most clearly evident at the MBA level – more about which follows later in the book.

Provide Space and Technology

Both of these elements do not differ significantly from the various potential structural models described in the undergraduate section earlier. Providing sufficient services for an increasingly international student population is challenging. In some cases, business schools just expect them to fit in with the majority of the local student population and thus do not offer much "tea and sympathy" to the differing needs of an international group. But even for schools in English-speaking environments, understanding the needs of international students or understanding what is actually going on in the school environment, is greatly aided if there is a sufficient language capacity among the staff such that some people speak whatever languages are significantly represented among the student body.

Graduate and Place Students

A similar challenge exists for career services. From the personal experience of one of the present authors who watched a move from an 80% domestic student population to a 95% international population over a 10-year period through the 1990s, it was a fascinating evolution. Initially, very few services were offered for international students. In terms of corporate relations and student placement, recruiting companies looked to the domestic, Dutch-speaking students as candidates. The international students were left to learn Dutch very quickly to try to identify international companies located in the Netherlands (where, in fact, English was often the corporate language) or to seek their fortunes on their own either in their own home countries or often in London.

The most difficult period was when the student population was evenly split between a group that wanted domestic contacts and another that sought international, English-speaking job opportunities. It was only when it was obvious that the school would develop and ultimately maintain an international orientation that student services, clearly incorporating career services, would have to reorient and match the students' language abilities and career destination desires as much as possible. That said, it remained impossible to provide services and for the school to be favoured by potential recruiters in all of the countries that the students had come from — Europe was alright but in the rest of the world, graduating perhaps a handful of students from Latin America, for example, hardly made one famous in Latin America.

Some years on, and especially after 9/11, the overall student service challenge for international students only increased as many countries brought in ever-more restrictive conditions for graduating students to receive post-study work visas in the country in which the school was located. This, in turn, has led to an eye-opening competition between nations on their perspective on how to act in a world of competition for talent.

At the small-minded end of the spectrum, at least at present, is the UK, which seems to be set on sending a significant number of intelligent graduating students away as soon as possible on graduation and has decreed that business schools and universities monitor student departures and are liable to ensure that they leave.

In the Asia region, Singapore is often viewed as an attractive place to live, work and study. The tightening of visas for foreign talent has had an adverse effect on placement for students who come to the island to study. This is especially true for pre-experience graduates as it is difficult for an employer to build a case for hiring a non-Singaporean. After graduation, students have a few months to seek local employment before they must leave the country. Universities in Singapore often remind international applicants that their programmes are not vehicles for immigrating to that small country. At the more open-minded end of the spectrum, Canada and Australia are much more generous in allowing students to seek and find employment after graduation. Each country, as mentioned, has its own approach.

Alumni Relations

Most business schools have become quite adept in managing alumni relations as this group of stakeholders can be a significant source for future funding. While not all alumni will be in a future position or have an interest in donating buildings, chaired faculty posts, or other significant contributions back to their alma mater, business schools work hard to establish a strong alumni following.

Instilling a strong sense of pride with alumni can aid in the marketing the school for future cohorts and even future generations. A strong alumni network can also be a great aid in the placement of graduates. We will address the impact of alumni relations in Chapter 5 as the nature and profile of the school has an impact on alumni relations and alumni giving.

Summary and Conclusions

In summary, the challenge for business schools is to assess the attractiveness of their home location for graduate students, develop uniqueness in the curriculum, manage the overall student population, including their skills and language abilities, and then build career services that fulfil, within reason and within budget constraints, an optimal approach for regional and international reach. For students without experience, the business school holds the promise of a solid and useful education and, ultimately, the prospects of gainful employment.

The analysis of the value chain for undergraduate and pre-experience student education in business schools highlights the array of services including housing, meals, technology, classrooms, and alumni relations. Within the general model of the business school there are many points of potential differentiation along the value chain, especially given the increasing international focus within and between schools.

The future of business school education for undergraduate and pre-experience master's students will likely continue to be anchored to the overall model of university education. Yet business schools will continue to be pressed to accelerate their international orientation while inculcating more practice-relevant skills to make their graduates competitive in the marketplace.

References

Chartered Association of Business Schools (2016, March). *UK business schools and international student recruitment: Trends, challenges and the case for change.* Retrieved September 2, 2017, from https://charteredabs.org/wp-content/uploads/2016/03/Chartered-ABS-International-Student-Recruitment-2016.pdf

Colby, A., Ehrlich, T., Sullivan, W. M., & Dolle, J. R. (2011). *Rethinking under-graduate business education: Liberal learning for the profession* (Vol. 20). San Francisco: John Wiley & Sons.

Commission on Institutions of Higher Education (CIHE). (n.d.). *U.S. regional accreditation: An overview.* Retrieved September 2, 2017, from https://cihe.neasc.org/about-accreditation/us-regional-accreditation-overview

Desilver, D. (2014, May). *5 facts about today's college graduates.* Retrieved September 2, 2017, from http://www.pewresearch.org/fact-tank/2014/05/30/5-facts-about-todays-college-graduates/

Education UK. (n.d.). *UK courses and qualifications delivered overseas.* Retrieved September 2, 2017, from http://www.educationuk.org/global/articles/uk-qualifications-overseas/

GVA. (2013). *Who owns student housing?* Retrieved September 2, 2017, from www.gva.co.uk/student-housing/who-owns-student-housing-winter-2013/

HESA. (2016). *Staff at higher education providers in the United Kingdom 2014/15.* Retrieved September 2, 2017, from https://www.hesa.ac.uk/news/21-01-2016/sfr225-staff

ICEF Monitor. (2014). *The agent question: New data has the answer.* Retrieved September 2, 2017, from http://monitor.icef.com/2014/09/the-agent-question-new-data-has-the-answer/

INTO. (n.d.). Retrieved September 2, 2017, from https://intoglobal.com/proven-impact#economic-and-community

Kollewe, J. (2016, January 30). *Rent bills high enough to make any student rebel.* Retrieved September 2, 2017, from https://www.theguardian.com/business/2016/jan/30/rent-bills-high-enough-student-rebel-accommodation-goldman-sachs

Navitas. (n.d.). Retrieved September 2, 2017, from https://www.navitas.com/partnerships

OBHE. (2014). *The agent question: Insights from students, universities, and agents* (Report by the Observatory on Borderless Higher Education). September 3.

Rivard, R. (2013, June 28). Exit at Embanet. *Inside Higher Education.* Retrieved September 2, 2017, from https://www.insidehighered.com/news/2013/06/28/after-pearson-deal-leaders-leaving-embanet

UK Council for International Student Affairs. (2016). *International student statistics: UK higher education.* Retrieved September 2, 2017, from http://institutions.ukcisa.org.uk//info-for-universities-colleges–schools/policy-research–statistics/research–statistics/international-students-in-uk-he/

Unite Group. (n.d.). *Who we are.* Retrieved September 4, 2017, from http://www.unite-group.co.uk/about-us/who-we-are

University Partnerships Programme. (n.d.). *Our portfolio.* Retrieved September 1, 2017, from http://www.upp-ltd.com/our-portfolio.php

U.S. Department of Education, National Center for Education Statistics. (2016). *Digest of education statistics, 2014* (NCES 2016-006) Chapter 3. Retrieved September 2, 2017, from http://nces.ed.gov/programs/digest/d15/tables/dt15_322.10.asp?current=yes

Chapter 3

Management Development (MBA, EMBA, Exec. Ed.)

Introduction

The undergraduate and pre-experience programmes share a number of important factors including admissions, student expectations, and placement. The MBA, EMBA, and Executive Education (Exec. Ed.) programmes are a bit of a different breed as the students have work experience and higher expectations. These expectations are not only related to the quality of the experience, but also related to the return on investment related to the fees and opportunity cost of attendance. As schools compete for students in these programmes, expectations seem to continue to increase around the world.

In this chapter, we will emphasize the unique considerations for the MBA, EMBA, and Executive Education programmes for the business school. We will cover the more strategic concerns, programme portfolio choices, and financial models in Chapters 4 and 5. We will start here with the MBA, one of the key hallmarks of the modern business school, yet one of the increasingly challenging programmes to deliver.

The MBA Value Chain

The MBA value chain is shown in Figure 3.1. The challenge of finding undergraduate and pre-experience students is, in most countries, simplicity itself compared to finding full-time MBA students. Where are they? Can they pay the often significant, MBA tuition fees? Are they smart enough to complete the course?

While marketing to undergraduate and pre-experience students is effectively business-to-consumer sales (as largely is MBA marketing, to be fair) there are major differences between them. Most notable is that important marketing channels to undergraduate and pre-experience student populations already exist either at secondary schools, national

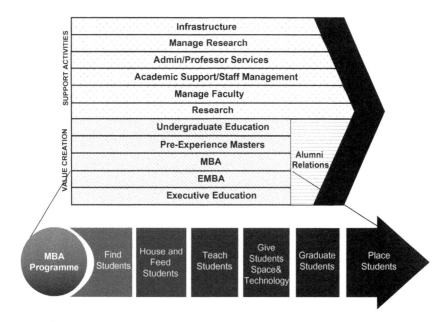

Figure 3.1.   Postgraduate Post-experience Education – MBA.

application services or while students are largely still at university for undergraduate studies.

Find Students

However, finding MBA students is much more challenging. MBA candidates will typically be working in entry-level or lower-middle management jobs normally with three to five years' work experience.

But there are some things a school can do proactively. The first driver for attracting potential MBAs is to achieve AACSB or EQUIS accreditation as that can be used as a differentiator. Accreditation is a must-have for business school looking to appear in rankings, certainly for the rankings published in the *Financial Times*. Rankings are the biggest overall driver of school attractiveness. In fact, MBA ranking is often seen as more important than research rankings for business schools (Trieschmann, Dennis, Northcraft, & Nieme, 2000). This is clearly the case for schools appearing in the top 20 of any of the major ranking – Bloomberg *Business Week*, the *Financial Times* and so on. Achieving success in accreditation or in the rankings is no mean feat, though.

Given that there are an estimated 13,000 business schools in the world, not all of them can appear in the top 20 of a ranking.

Beyond playing the rankings game, business schools do their best to market via traditional print media or online through Google Adwords or through more specific social media channels — often with a "call to action" of attending an open day at the school or an introductory session at a location somewhere around the world. The aim is to meet candidates and to attempt to convince them of the suitability of a particular school. Candidate MBA fairs provide another channel to recruit potential students but they can be difficult as each individual school is surrounded by competitor schools pitching their own benefits.

Fairs also generate mailing lists of candidates, as does GMASS, the Graduate Management Admissions Council's database of GMAT test-takers or those interested in business schools. About 400,000 candidates are registered and willing to be contacted each recruitment cycle — an opt-in rate of about 75% of the candidates. Schools that require the GMAT for admission can purchase access to these candidates for 75 cents per name (2016 price) and send emails to these candidates.

Schools make use of such a service by identifying and targeting attractive individual candidates through to highly sophisticated all-in campaigns more akin to heavy consumer marketing than the historically gentler and often not all that sophisticated approach more normal in higher education. But convincing MBA candidates to become MBA students means more than getting them interested. It is also a contracting arrangement and, as in any contract, negotiations form an integral part of the deal. The question of return on investment of the MBA degree is also often on the minds of students though studies have shown mixed results on the value of holding an MBA (Dreher, Dougherty, & Whitely, 1985).

That caveat aside, and focusing on business schools in the West (where experience suggest there are more MBA places available than students to fill them), candidates seek scholarships, discounts, soft loans and access to other types of loans from banks or from national providers. Our experience is that the overall proportion of students who pay full tuition is much lower than one would think in an esteemed and societally vital service such as providing education. It has become, for better or worse, a marketplace.

Schools seek to balance recruiting the best possible candidates with candidates who can actually pay the tuition and who are in some cases simply "OK" while simultaneously managing overall classroom yields. A full class of 60 or 70 MBA students, all of whom have paid as much as the school hopes for, is financially more viable than a class of 12 or 20 or 25 outstanding candidates that have had to be discounted significantly to get them to come at all.

Thus, between the cost of marketing to create awareness of the school in the first place and then the cost of the negotiation and the discounts offered in the second place, the full-time MBA market, while highly prestigious in the minds of the broad business school community, can actually be lucrative or penurious for schools. It is increasingly becoming a "winner takes all" competition. The top 20 in the business school rankings can turn candidates away. Those further down the rankings (or not in them at all) may scramble and struggle every year to recruit a class. From a business school perspective, the full-time MBA market is the hardest market of all to compete in successfully.

However, many schools located in a metropolitan area have been quite successful with part-time MBA programmes that allow working professionals to complete the degree during weekends or evenings. A part-time programme can offer the same classes as its full-time version over a longer duration and allow students to avoid a lengthy period without employment. Many part-time students still wish to use the MBA degree as a catalyst for career growth and even a potential career change. The challenge with many of the part-time MBA programmes is finding faculty who are willing to teach on evenings and at weekends.

House and Feed Students

It is hard to say where the tipping point where students consider themselves customers as much as students exactly is. Does it begin with undergraduate students or with postgraduate pre-experience students or with MBAs? Is it a factor of fee levels and thus dependent on a particular school? Whatever the case, there is little doubt that full-time MBA students regularly consider themselves customers who have bought an expensive learning and social experience in which they state quite openly that they expect proper accommodation, classroom quality, break-out room space, computer and internet access, excellent Wi-Fi and decent food. (Baldwin, Bedell, & Johnson, 1997). Nowhere is this more apparent than in MBA housing. Whether business school housing is managed in-house or in a joint venture, accommodation standards continue to increase and room size continues to expand.

Once at school, the demands often manifest themselves in a sort of apartheid. In many cases, MBA housing is provided in graduate-only student accommodation. Teaching takes place in similarly restricted classrooms in reserved wings of a building or even in entirely separate buildings from the undergraduate "hordes". It really does depend on whether a business school is primarily about graduate programmes or whether the MBA programme is a "flagship" among other activities. In the former case, separation from others can be unnecessary – except perhaps from pre-experience "youngsters". In the latter case, significant expenditure has taken place to provide expensive and expansive teaching facilities for MBAs.

Teach Students

Compared to the expectations and requirements of pre-experience master's students, suffice it to say that in the MBA everything is upped a notch or two. On the teaching side, with MBA students in full-on customer mode, there is little patience among students for faculty who are not lively in the classroom, who do not speak "decent" English or who are too academic and not "practical" enough. Academics and staff have more than once heard students calculate their per hourly "listening cost" of something above $125 in many schools and to let management know that such-and-such a professor's three- hour class was not worth $375.

So, business schools need to decide how to staff these programmes. Using excessive numbers of part-time or visiting faculty can be disadvantageous. Faculty can become very virtualised by visiting staff, who are often academic teaching professionals, or business practitioners who teach on the side. Students may in many cases be happy with their teaching experience but once the teaching contingent has become too virtualised schools can get into trouble with accreditation bodies, which expect most faculty members teaching on degree programmes to be structurally tied to the school, to be academically qualified to doctoral level, and to be actively researching and publishing. The logical end game here is that accreditation is endangered or not achieved. This in turn affects the ability to be in the rankings – where a poor business school performance can wreak havoc in perceptions of quality among students.

Graduate and Place Students

Providing career services to MBA students is again similar to the experience of pre-experience students but this time on steroids. To help pave the way for career placement, many MBA programmes encourage internships as a way of providing additional work experience for students. These internships may be paid or completed for credit as a part of the programme requirements. Obviously, it allows the employers to "preview" the MBA candidates and can lead to higher placement rates. Alumni relations is typically more aggressive and engaged for MBA programmes as the cohort experience and class network is much stronger than it is for undergraduates.

The Executive MBA Value Chain

The Executive MBA programme is a hinge point of sorts for many schools between the world of students and degree programmes and the world of executive education. In some schools, the EMBA is managed in conjunction with other degree programmes as the value chain (shown in Figure 3.2) appears to be similar. This makes sense from one angle – the EMBA is effectively a part-time MBA with he same or very similar content and is simply scheduled in a way that makes it possible for working professionals to study. On the other hand, because the

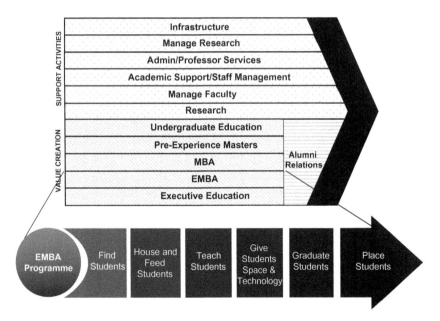

Figure 3.2.   Postgraduate Post-experience Education – Executive MBA.

students, or "participants", are working professionals, the EMBA is considered part of executive education.

Assuming that the issue of the home of the EMBA is a question of semantics would be a misguided conclusion. Where the programme is located within a school has a very real effect on who is managing the programme, what the service levels are, who teaches on the programme and so forth. The present authors consider the EMBA a part of the degree programme portfolio as we feel that the academic considerations of the EMBA must be supported and maintained and that that is more sensibly done within a broad degree programme department or approach. This is not a hard and fast rule or requirement though.

Find Students

Finding EMBA students is strongly affected by the actual structure of the programme and a variety of models of the EMBA provision exist. Most typically, programmes are delivered on one or two evenings per week, a design is suited to large urban areas – either in city centres or suburbs that are heavily populated with corporate offices. Participants can go directly from office to classroom. There are some real advantages to this design but there are also drawbacks. The advantage is educational – participants learn continuously, in smaller blocks, at a location close to their place of work and home, which saves them accommodation and travel costs. On the downside, blocking out an evening or two per week for a two-year period is very difficult to align for working professionals who travel for their work. Additionally, it is easy to skip a class because of deadlines or other work-related engagements.

From a school's perspective, a part-time evening MBA is a bet on finding sufficient numbers of commuter students so that the classroom can be filled. Given that filling classrooms is a big challenge for all but the most prestigious schools anyway, the week/night model is probably not the most attractive option.

The second variation is a model that, in one form or another, straddles weekends, everything from Friday evening and all day Saturday every second week through to four-day weekends once a month, each providing around 500 contact hours over a two-year period. Finally, there is the one-whole-week every two months EMBA programme. If the weekday model aims at car commuters, the weekend model additionally aims at low-cost flight participants, who can realistically consider a school up to an hour or two flight away from their homes. The distance students will consider travelling really depends on the prestige of the institution. From our own experience, students will cross continents for programmes that they consider really attractive.

Having looked at where recruitment needs to take place geographically for differing programme formats, the actual question of recruitment arises. For schools requiring the GMAT for their EMBA programme, turning to GMASS is an option. Beyond that, a school needs to think through how to market in business to business consumer terms. It is ultimately the individual participant who wants to study on the programme but the individual wants his or her employer to pay as much of the tuition as possible. The "customer" for the school is thus a combination of the individual and the company and a school has to sell the benefits of an EMBA to the employer via the candidate or, if possible, directly. This not only means selling the benefits of the programme to an organisation's management but also informing them of all of the financing options and tax implications.

It is also possible to adjust the sales channel by trying to sell to the "business" directly, with the goal of encouraging the training and development department to select an individual or group of individuals annually to join a consortium of organisations that each puts forward five or six participants annually or to commission a complete programme for themselves.

House and Feed Students

Given that EMBA participants are generally speaking middle managers in their 30s or early 40s, providing them with accommodation and hospitality is much more like providing services to executives than to students. Benchmarking, in participants' eyes, is with other venues that they attend for corporate events: conference centres, business travel hotels, nice restaurants – rather than with a student experience of low-service minimalism. Some business schools have their own conference centre accommodation that is used for EMBA students as well as for executive education participants. In other cases, deals are made with local hotels or in urban business schools a range of accommodation is suggested.

Teach Students

Given their profile as working professionals, EMBAs seek as much if not more practicality from their degree studies than do MBAs. They are studying in order to gain knowledge and to be able to add "MBA" to their educational experience but mostly they are studying in order to progress their careers while simultaneously juggling their studies with day jobs and family responsibilities. EMBAs thus seek to be able to apply their studies as quickly and as successfully in their own organisations in order to be promoted to the next level of responsibility. In many cases, this means progressing from a more technical or specifically delineated role to a more general management role where managing people, rather than managing knowledge or expertise, becomes central.

Teaching EMBAs thus becomes a task where the students look for concrete organisational experience from faculty members rather than academic and research experience. However, given the intermittent scheduling of EMBA programmes, whether in the evenings, over weekends or in blocks, schools often turn to visiting faculty to teach.

Provide Space and Technology

Where possible, business schools prefer students come to campus to create the right student learning experience. However, delivering EMBA programmes, certainly those taught in blocks, is a relatively simple "product" to export. A school effectively needs only a teaching room, some break out rooms, and somewhere to house and feed the students and the faculty members teaching them. Commitments to requisite facilities can be annual, rather than multi-year, to keep costs under control and flexible. The challenge is to find appropriate, reasonably priced and technologically sophisticated locations for the programme.

Graduate and Place Students

As in previous sections of this chapter, the same set of options for MBA graduates applies also to EMBA students in terms of degree-awarding processes. The most obvious advantage of EMBA participants is that they are generally not looking for jobs but more for career advancement (Petit, 2011). To accomplish this, career coaching is the most requested service. Where schools do, however, need to make a decision is on whether or not to open up overall career services to EMBA students. What they decide can be anything and everything from a total ban on participation, hard-to-enforce rules that only self-financing EMBA students have access to career services through to a self-managed approach where EMBAs are left to judge for themselves on whether it is ethical to actively search for a new job while being financed by a current employer. In practice, many EMBA graduates are promoted to new roles within their own organisations but a significant minority change jobs or use the EMBA programme as a launch pad for their own businesses, often in an area related to their fields of expertise in their previous job. Like the MBA programme, the effort on alumni relations typically becomes more engaging and active quickly since the cohort and network effect is quite strong. EMBA graduates are likely to be in a strong position to contribute to the school by helping with placement of undergraduates, creating ties to industry, and potentially for future donations to the endowment.

In summary, the EMBA programme, even more so than full-time programmes, has many opportunities for substitution and for virtualisation. With the exception of student recruitment services, which tend not to be extensively involved in the EMBA market and remain a responsibility of the school, housing and feeding students, teaching students and providing them with classrooms and break-out space can be extensively outsourced. The school's job, and the focus of external quality assurance processes, is to ensure that the level of education is truly at master's level, that the faculty are suitable and that, especially for satellite-based activities, the overall student experience is what it should be.

The Executive Education Value Chain

The emphasis so far has been on examining and summarising the processes, similarities and differences of the MBA and EMBA programme value chains. Now the focus turns to executive education.

Here again there are significant differences in many of the elements of the value chain as shown in Figure 3.3. However, the overarching value chain of executive education is significantly different from the processes that are at play in degree programmes.

In many ways, open programmes or short courses are the realm in which executive education is most easily understood. Courses have a stated theme and a pre-designed curriculum; they are scheduled and so can be staffed ahead of time and are thus "products" like degree programmes rather than "services" in the custom programme realm.

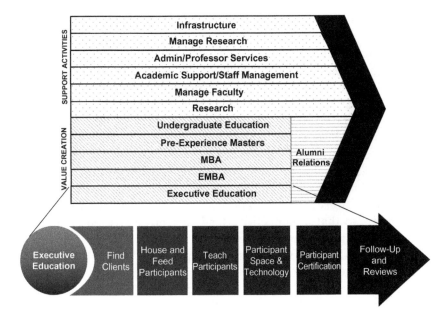

Figure 3.3. Postgraduate Post-experience Education — Executive Education.

Find Participants

While it is very straight-forward to design a three-day or a two-week open programme, finding participants for these programmes is often very hard work. Business schools know little beyond the fact that potential participants will be working managers. They can be located anywhere and in any organisation that can afford the price tag attached to an open programme — generally somewhere in the range of $1,000 to $1,500 or equivalent per day of attendance.

The most obvious starting point for thinking through a sales strategy is to advertise physically or virtually in newspapers or magazines or through an online channel. The problem here, however, is that advertising is expensive. And while programmes can be lucrative on the basis of each taught day, the fact that most programmes are very short means they are not as lucrative overall in comparison to, say, an EMBA programme.

The second path to market is to "work" contacts, including past participants and as many learning and development professionals as possible. Big providers of open programmes, whether business schools or professional training organisations, will have databases of tens, if not hundreds or thousands, of names often supplemented by additional bought-in mailing lists. For schools new to the activity there is clearly an entry-barrier here. Accumulating a sufficiently large mailing list by either making it or buying it is an expensive process. Acquiring the skill set to continuously work a database with a sufficient range of "products" – different open programmes to sell - is also a challenge. Matching the right potential audience with the right course exacerbates the process even further. One can either specifically target potential participants directly or hope that the corporate learning and development function within a target organisation will work as a clearing house. Some organisations will only approve certain potential providers of open courses so that a competitive tendering process is required and a business school must jump through a whole range of "hoops" simply to be approved and then hope that something actually comes out of all of the effort involved.

Where processes work in favour of a school, deals are made where a relationship is formed between the school and the learning and development function leading to multiple participants on a programme. This is sometimes taken a step further so that an organisation's participants are brought together additionally to top and tail their participation.

In addition to the challenges of selling open programmes, there is the task of making a school's programmes distinctive and innovative. Creating programmes that can really make a significant impact and difference for participants can be quite difficult (de Vries & Korotov, 2007). Because most faculty focus on the design, it is all too often forgotten how hard it is to sell programmes. In addition, programmes tend to pop up from various points within a business school and not solely from within a centralised open programmes team within an executive education department. Different departments, and in some cases individual faculty members, regularly feel that they "own" a programme and are entitled to design it as they see fit, to run it as they see fit, and to keep the revenues for their own departmental or individual rather than school goals.

On top of that, business schools are regularly approached by third parties who want to run an open programme together with the school. Sometimes the approach will come from another business school and in other cases from training providers or professional associations. Assessing whether these approaches are worth pursuing is challenging. Invariably, discussions will take place about roles and responsibilities. Business plans are developed, usually in best-case scenarios, where both parties get rich and live happily ever after. In reality, assigning responsibilities and revenue sharing or profit sharing agreements are not easy. It is difficult enough to make money within a single school from open programmes. Working together means that revenue must be even higher to ensure multiple parties feel the process is worthwhile.

In partnership arrangements, or within a single school setting, the next hurdle is whether a programme will actually run as there will always be one that does not have the sought-after number of participants some weeks before it is scheduled to take place. Two considerations need to be taken. The first ought to be whether the participant experience will be of sufficient quality. A course with seven delegates is probably not the ideal experience although schools are surprisingly flexible in telling participants that they will have an extremely enjoyable experience with personal attention and tender loving care when numbers are looking decidedly small.

The second consideration that tends to dominate is whether it is financially worth running the programme and, relatedly, if a decision is made to cancel the iteration whether delegates can be persuaded to reschedule and turn up for the next time the programme is to run. From many school's perspectives, cancelling is undesirable. The faculty member's time has been committed and finding a substitute activity is next to impossible.

House and Feed Participants

There is little to add to the description of EMBA participants outlined earlier in terms of accommodation and hospitality. The only element worth noting that has not been addressed earlier is that additional attention to cultural sensitivity is often required from a school. Open programme participants often attend from a whole range of different countries, as indeed do degree programme students. Ensuring that dietary requirements are catered for, that prayer schedules are incorporated, that Ramadan is considered and that gender relations are understood can be a significant task.

Teach Participants

Unlike degree programmes, open programmes and executive education do not have the same underlying requirement for faculty qualifications and research activity. While some schools work on the basis of only using resident faculty, others end up developing executive education faculty who are distinct from the "academic" faculty or work with a significant proportion of external faculty members. Who is suited to teach depends very much on the content of a programme. Advanced, cutting-edge finance programmes will feature research-active faculty members in a way that open programmes based on leadership and coaching will not. Either way, teaching tends to be externally focused insofar as faculty members will use examples and case studies that will make sense for all of the participants but not focus specifically on the organisations of the attendees. Examples will be sought but, generally, open programmes are "generic".

An additional point to mention (often overlooked) is that executive education, including open programmes, customised programmes and also the EMBA, are in many cases an "unnatural" form of education compared to traditional degree programmes. Teaching non-stop, and listening to teachers non-stop, from 9:00 until 20:00 often for several consecutive days is exhausting and not really all that great for learning. It thus falls on the programme design team to ensure that there is a mix of activities rather than straightforward teaching. This requires a sophisticated approach from faculty members, too, who must ensure that there is a lot of class participation, plenty of break-out groups and that consideration is given to experiential activities, simulations and other forms of learning.

Provide Space and Technology

Open programme participants have a similar demographic and expectations to EMBA students. Spatial requirements really depend on the type of programme as well as the number of participants. Where the content is more teachable, and the group size is larger, traditional horseshoe-style classrooms tend to be used. This is not ideal, however, when group work is required and participants expect more attention and involvement. At that point, flat classrooms, set up "cabaret-style" with groups of six or so participants sitting around a table, are more suitable. Many seating arrangements are ultimately possible and we have seen programmes with participants on beanbags, sitting outside in a garden under trees, or walking and talking for substantial periods of time.

Certify Participants

In most cases, certification takes place with certificates being handed out at the end of a programme and, depending on where participants are from, a lot of photos being taken or not. In other cases, however, business schools have developed pathway programmes where the open programme is part of an academically certificated process that garners a certain number of academic credits. There are also a number of open programmes that will lead to discounting for a more substantial subsequent programme. The latter approach is not particularly hard to manage. The former is more of a challenge because academically certifying a programme means ensuring that the content is at an appropriate, generally master's, level; that there is a proper assessment regime; and that assignments are completed and graded. When all participants in an open programme are on a path to academic certification, this is easier. When a small number of participants are seeking academic credit while others are not, an imbalance can quickly arise as participants do not take the programme equally seriously.

Follow Up

The goal of attending an educational intervention, especially for professionals who are taken out of their workplace for the experience, is of course to apply the new skills and insights they have acquired back in that workplace. This learning transfer is, however, not automatic, largely for three reasons.

The first is that the participant re-enters a culture that has established ways of doing things and "new ideas" do not always go over well. The second is that work tends to overwhelm a returning participant when the tsunami backlog of email hits and the participant just falls back into his or her previous pattern. The third is that learning takes time to flourish. New insights, or different ways of doing things – especially more people-based ways of doing things – take time to embed. The neuroscience of learning basically says repeat, repeat, practice, practice, practice.

The best approach that a business school can take is to build follow-up into the programme design. In a perfect world, this would mean additional face-to-face elements some time after the first intervention, either through a modular programme design or through a follow-up event or a follow-up coaching session. Where that is not possible, technologically facilitated synchronous sessions using Skype, WebEx or the old fashioned telephone or asynchronous emails or other approaches can be used.

Within the continuum of business school education ranging from undergraduate through to open programmes in executive education, there are many differences at each stage but similarities are also recognisable. The path to market is either business to consumer or business-to-business consumer. Teaching is largely content-based. Activities are scheduled and pre-arranged and can be written up and described in a brochure. Financially, a school can calculate income and costs, as a factor of participant numbers and each additional participant is marginal profit.

Custom Executive Education

Custom executive education is an entirely different type of offering and there are two distinct types of custom programme: customised learning and development; and customised organisational development.

Although exact delineation is impossible, learning and development interventions are programmes in which a content-led schedule is developed in the course of the design process; in an organisational development intervention, the primarily emphasis is on process, rather than content design. This will be further explained below.

Find Clients

The competition in executive education for custom programmes is increasing around the world (Czinkota & Johansson, 2015). It is therefore critical to have an aggressive and talented sales team in place to build a pipeline of potential clients. In a learning and development sales process, the primary client is "the organisation". Defining what that means in practice is not always clear as "an organisation" is, in executive education parlance, a "social construct of conversation". Deciding whom to have the conversation with generally leads in the direction of the head of learning and development, sometimes in the human resources function within the potential client organisation and sometimes reporting directly to the "C" level, often in the guise of a Chief Learning Officer who is sometimes also the head of the corporate university.

In other cases, conversations can take place with the chief executive directly. It is tempting to think that the task of developing an organisation's people capacity, the "talent", would loom large on the agenda of the CEO. Sometimes this is indeed the case but it is far from ubiquitous. In other cases, conversations take place with a line manager.

The conversations tend to be different in each of the above scenarios. When talent development is discussed with the learning and development functions, the conversations tend to be about organisation-wide initiatives: developing "high-potential" talent, creating better leadership capacity, and understanding and working within a globalised workforce.

However, if the conversation takes place with the CEO, the discussion turns to aligning the overall organisation with the organisational strategy so that there is a shared view of priorities, of the mission, vision and, importantly, finances for the upcoming period.

Finally, if the discussion involves line managers, it is often to address a specific, more contained need: typical examples include working with the finance department to get them to better understand the opportunities and risks rather than "being bean counters" or rolling out a training programme to improve the business to business sales skills within the sales and marketing functions in industrial businesses.

Getting to these conversations is a task in and of itself. Business schools can proactively seek out discussion partners by directly visiting target organisations or by attending events where learning and development people congregate. In the latter case, a whole conference industry has emerged in recent years specifically to match companies "with a learning and development budget" with potential service providers. The service providers pay to attend and the companies tend to be invited for free. More than once, business school representatives will have found themselves not speaking, as they had hoped for, to a senior, budget-holding learning and development professional but with someone lower down the organisation who has been sent to attend as a cross between a "recce" (an intelligence process) and a "jolly" (a reward for performance).

Successful proactive discussions do not tend to lead to anything much in the short term. The business-to-business sales process is about relationship building where multiple points of contact are required and years can go by without a financial transaction of any sort taking place. The business school will then eventually invite contacts that exist and new contacts that have been made to open days featuring faculty members showcasing their knowledge and abilities.

Managing the process of proactively visiting potential clients and then "keeping them warm" means that schools need the appropriate staffing to accomplish these two goals. Conversations tend to be conducted by learning and development specialists in business schools, many of whom will have come from the corporate side originally as purchasers of executive education as much as by being faculty members. Managing the on-going process tends to be provided by a combination of sales and marketing in-house staff, database teams and corporate communications specialists. The infrastructure for success in executive education is considerable and generally expensive.

For schools that have built a reputation for executive education, the second element of the sales process is the reactive component of following up on enquiries and requests for help from within the contact network or sometimes additionally through posted RFIs (requests for information) or RFPs (requests for proposals) on public procurement websites. For larger operations, dozens of requests can come in every week. Sifting through the requests, deciding which to pursue and subsequently responding to them is again very time and effort intensive.

RFIs and RFPs will be sent out to many potential suppliers. In a successful process, a business school will get on the long list of potential suppliers through the RFI, which describes the school's skills, track record and often the financial history. That then allows the school to make a more specific proposal, ideally in a proper discussion with the potential client although that is by no means guaranteed, to then get on to a short list. Short-listed business schools will then be invited to present their proposals at a beauty parade of a small number of potential suppliers.

Looking at this from the staffing perspective, the content and financial attractiveness of an RFI needs to be screened by someone with considerable experience; proposal documents need to be prepared by a bid team along with contractual elements − either at this point in the process or later. The RFI generally needs to be reviewed from a legal point of view; and the "pitch team" needs to include not only the client relationship manager but also faculty members and/or specialised adjuncts and associates of the school, who are most likely to actually be teaching on the programme. It is critical that a team of three or four attend a pitch to show the client that one is serious and values the potential business.

So far so good but this stage in the process is not the time to break out the champagne because another hurdle will often be thrown up. A business school will have achieved preferred bidder status, which will allow it to further refine content elements of their proposal and often be asked to re-calculate costs in a downward direction in preparation for subsequent discussions with the dreaded procurement department. Here they will be told that other bidders in the process will have come from large consultancies, from boutique learning and development houses and – this has happened – even from their own faculty.

Business schools that understand this process will be cognisant of a number of important financial variables. Lowering the overall price can be achieved by shortening a programme or by taking additional nice-to-have elements out of the proposal. Lowering the per-participant cost can be achieved most readily by proposing that the target number of participants be increased from, for example, 24 attendees to 30 attendees, which will drop the per-person cost by 20%.

Having come to a contractual agreement, the business school's executive education team will be pleased, notwithstanding the regret that they have been haggled down to a price point that is not as attractive as they had originally hoped for. But so be it. An announcement will be made within the school that a large contract has been won with a particular organisation that will provide "20 iterations of a programme over the next two years to a prestigious partner" worth "large amounts of money". In happy circumstances, this will all go according to plan. In unhappy circumstances, of which there are plenty, the original best intentions of delivering 20 iterations is whittled down to delivering four iterations because of – choose one here – recession, terrorism, bird flu, ash clouds, snow storms, typhoons, change of ownership, departure of the organisation's learning and development contact, a new CEO who seeks to "wipe the slate clean and start again", a lack of participants from the organisation because they are busy, a lack of clarity on who pays within the organisation between learning and development and the operating companies, an election, a new government in China, an oil price crash and so on. Discussions will take place within the business school on whether it can attempt to get the client to live up to the original contract. This tends to come to nothing. Suing your clients for breach of contract tends to mean they will not come back again in the future and still won't pay anyway.

The last element to touch upon about the overall client acquisition side is that it is very lumpy. There are potentially large deals and small ones, short-term ones and longer-running ones. There are more lucrative ones and less financially attractive ones (Hura, 2003). Demand for proposals has peaks and troughs. Requests for programme content are highly unpredictable. Custom executive education has much more to do with the service offering of a professional services firm that it does with the traditional concept of what a business school does. It's a very different business!

House and Feed Participants

The accommodation and hospitality requirements for open programme participants were described earlier. There is little difference in the expectations voiced by participants on customised programmes since the demographics are largely similar. Worth noting is that custom programmes often attract senior members of the client organisation – not necessarily as participants but as guest speakers. An organised business school will ensure additional service levels and also do its best to build deeper client relationships with top management.

What a business school will also find is that custom clients increasingly ask it to deliver programme iterations in different locations around the world that are convenient to the clients' needs. Thus a business school will need to be able to deliver and ensure high standards of accommodation and hospitality whether it be at a hotel, the school, wherever the client has chosen or at a corporate university location.

Teach Participants

Teaching participants on custom programmes, when done well, is a completely different approach from teaching in more generic situations. The stated purpose of the client organisation, after all, is to maximise the value of the learning to its multiple needs. To achieve this, faculty members need to move beyond teaching their usual material or case studies as they might for a degree or open programme.

While faculty members will know a lot about their own area of expertise, participants will know infinitely more about their own organisations. The challenge, then, is to find a judicious balance between academic content, outside examples and other novel elements and teasing-out and working with the knowledge that the participants have and the challenges that they are working on. For a faculty member this means having both content knowledge and excellent skills in working with delegates. In practice, it also means that the clients, whatever they may say, are not looking for cutting-edge academic research but an academically sound, innovative but practical and not overly sophisticated content design.

Again, while some business schools field only their full-time academics for custom programmes, most will have "pracademics" – hybrid faculty members with both academic and external organisational experience – to do much of the teaching. This is not only because of the content and facilitation required for successful executive education (which very few full-time academics have) but also because of very practical scheduling complications. Degree programmes are products with a pre-determined curriculum and related schedules; custom programmes are projects with a shorter time line and much more of a pop-up schedule. A full-time academic who is committed for years ahead to a teaching schedule with classes on Tuesday mornings and Thursday afternoons is often not in a position to fly around the globe to satisfy the requirements of a custom programme.

Business schools with extensive custom executive education activities have long rosters of learning experts, associate pracademics, visiting faculty from other schools and straight-up practitioners. They will have coaches on their books plus a little black book of interesting, amusing and hopefully successful experiential learning activities that can feature drummers, actors and musicians and involve changing tyres on Formula One racing cars, facilitated computer-based simulations and, in one memorable and expensive example, a multi-day learning journey based on Odysseus' adventures in Homer's *The Odyssey*, plus the recreation of a Niger Delta village in New York for an oil company executive education programme.

There is a growing trend towards incorporating project-based learning, or action learning, into custom programmes (Ye, Van Os, Chapman, & Jacobson, 2017). As mentioned earlier, retention and real application of learning is often a challenge in executive education. By taking a project-based approach, there is a bridge across the gap between "work" and "class". These projects can pose an additional challenge – finding faculty capable of coaching or consulting student project teams working on real company issues (Jacobson, Chapman, Ye, & Os, 2017). Because of the significant time and focus required this is generally left to part-time consultants or adjuncts.

Provide Space and Technology

As with accommodation, teaching space expectations are high. Flat classrooms predominate, as horseshoe shaped teaching spaces are not well suited to groups of senior executives.

From a technology perspective, the situation is similar: preparatory registration and learning materials; on-going access to Wi-Fi to support the learning experience (and allow the checking of emails while on the programme); and synchronous or asynchronous follow-up are expected. Where there is an apparent need for business schools to be service-minded is when learning materials need to be integrated into the corporate learning zones. While this should, in theory, be relatively simple, in practice security levels on some corporate networks are sometimes so severe that getting access to material is difficult. Business schools, together with IT experts on the client side, then need to get material behind the firewall. From our experience, this occurs more often with public-sector clients than it does with corporates. It really depends on the business that the client is in, however, and the security levels deemed necessary and appropriate.

Certify Participants and Follow Up

Both of these stages in the value chain have been described previously in the section on open programmes. The significant difference, of course, is that custom programmes generally have attendees from a single organisation and discussions about the need to certify are simpler because they can be conducted with the learning and development team.

There is an interesting market for single companies that deserves a short mention. While certifying very short interventions, which could only gain a small number of credits, is generally not required, and getting companies to commit to entire degree programmes requires very significant dedication, there is a demand – certainly in the UK – for postgraduate certificates and postgraduate diplomas. The former is officially recognised as one-third of a master's degree and the latter two-thirds of a master's. From a business school perspective, this is interesting because it allows participants to continue on to further stages of a master's degree – even if the original sponsoring organisation does not wish to support them directly. This qualification and its mobility for qualification for further stages can be very attractive.

Organisation Development Activities

Pure-play organisation development (OD) interventions are comparatively rare. In most cases, OD elements form a part of a learning and development intervention.

For the sake of clarity, OD is best defined as a "planned and systematic approach to enabling sustained organizational performance through the involvement of its people" (Chartered Institute of Personnel and Development [CIPD], 2016).

In practice, an OD intervention is where facilitators expedite a conversation-based process with an organisation's participants in contrast to teaching them. There are a number of different OD approaches that draw on sociology, psychology, and theories of motivation and engagement. This contrasts significantly from the learning and development approach of the transfer of skills and knowledge. OD interventions are particularly appropriate in situations where significant change is required or, alternatively, when a merger or acquisition has taken place and a new holistic, strategically focused culture needs to emerge from two legacy organisations. These programmes can provide a strong partnership arrangement between businesses and the business school (Ghoshal, Arnzen, & Brownfield, 1992).

Find Clients

As a conceptual aid, one can consider learning and development interventions as "chronic" needs that will continue long into the future. There will always be high-potential employees who need to be developed. There will always be a need for non-financial managers to better understand finances. There will always be a need for better general management and leadership. OD, in contrast, can be characterised as an "acute" need where an intervention is essential "right here and right now" because of change issues due to mergers and acquisitions or strategic realignments.

Due to the acute nature of these interventions, they will have sponsorship from the most senior levels of an organisation, even if the actual RFP selection process will often be conducted by someone in HR, learning and development or sometimes within a specific OD department in the organisation. While there are generally individuals within business schools who subscribe to an OD world view because they have come to the business school from a psychology background rather than from a teaching perspective, few traditional business schools have extensive capacities in this field. Competition tends to come from specialist boutiques and from some specialised business schools. The actual RFI/RFP process is very similar to the custom programme stages described earlier. There is obviously a difference in the terminology and in the conversation that is held with the client as it is based on psychology and can appear completely alien to traditional business school academics as well as to traditional business people.

The key difference, however, is that pricing is based on service days worked on a *per diem* model. This makes sense because there is not a three-day programme delivered 20 times but there is a package of work that is more fluid and involves one-to-one meetings, extensive smaller group workshops, large group events, communications management and so on.

Scoping the package of work is impossible for a business school to do by itself. It requires complete "co-makership" with the client organisation and a collaborative approach to delivery that builds in review points to consider whether additional interventions or stages are required.

House and Feed Client Participants

OD interventions, given their multi-faceted nature, tend to take place not only in specific conference or classroom settings but also in the workplace. Thus, with the exception of the larger group events, there are fewer venue considerations for business schools to make.

Teach Client Participants

Teaching is a misnomer for most OD interventions. It is more appropriate to view these engagements as facilitated events based on an overall framework and schedule but otherwise emergent. As participant group sizes increase so too does the need for additional facilitators. It is not unusual to have a team of half-a-dozen or more facilitators at work simultaneously and large group events where 20 facilitators, from both a business school and the client organisation, may be working together. The skill set, as indicated by the types of conversations that take place in an OD intervention, are significantly different from traditional or executive education teaching.

Conducting a largely unscripted conversation often over many days using theoretical frameworks that require the bulk of the input to come from participants is a specific and very challenging skill. Conversations must be allowed to meander but they also need to be directed towards finding common ground and agreement where possible, while parking disagreement on the side. Facilitators, as mentioned earlier, tend to have backgrounds in organisational psychology rather than in business disciplines.

OD interventions, as with custom interventions, are also project-based and "lumpy". The demand for OD is unpredictable and thus having facilitators available involves a combination of a smaller in-house availability – or in some cases no in-house availability – and a large contingent of adjuncts and associates. In either case, scheduling a group of facilitators, especially when interventions scale up, is a challenge and requires a thick "little black book" as well as the ability to create a team of facilitators who can work together seamlessly and efficiently.

Certifying Participants and Follow Up

In general, certifying OD interventions is not really appropriate. Given the nature of an OD intervention, follow-up should be built into the overall design. Ensuring that change becomes embedded requires not only individual but also group follow-up.

Summary and Conclusions

This chapter reviewed the value chains for the MBA, EMBA and executive education offerings in business schools. These programmes challenge the traditional university model as students are more like paying customers with high expectations. As such, there are a number of important considerations of not only what happens inside the classroom but also outside with dining, lodging and other student experiences.

At the same time, the number of full-time MBA students is declining and competition is rising, which is creating an unsustainable position for some schools. Some institutions may be successful with part-time MBA offerings, provided there are large numbers of working professionals in the immediate vicinity. However, the sustainability of the full-time MBA along with the EMBA may be a question for many schools in the future.

Executive education has grown significantly in the past decade as organisations and individuals look for ways to build skills and capabilities. Open programmes can be quite difficult to design and market in a way that has targeted impact yet have wide appeal. Custom executive education programmes must be designed thoughtfully and generally require strong client relationship management capabilities. Organisation development (OD) offerings require significant planning and a strong partnership between a business school and the business teams. OD programmes are often difficult for a business school to secure due to the increasing number of consulting firms playing in the executive education space. Business schools must carefully consider these offerings when evaluating their portfolios and make strategic decisions that fit the situation and market.

References

Baldwin, T. T., Bedell, M. D., & Johnson, J. L. (1997). The social fabric of a team-based M.B.A. program: Network effects on student satisfaction and performance. *Academy of Management Journal, 40*(6), 1369–1397.

Chartered Institute of Personnel and Development. (2016). *Organisation development /fact sheet*. Retrieved 2 September, 2017 from http://www.cipd.co.uk/hr-resources/factsheets/organisation-development.aspx#

Czinkota, M. R., & Johansson, J. K. (2015). Competition in executive education: A global marketing perspective. In E. Wilson & W. Black (Eds.), *Proceedings of the 1994 Academy of Marketing Science (AMS) Annual Conference*, pp. 154–158. Springer, Cham: Springer International Publishing.

de Vries, M. K., & Korotov, K. (2007). Creating transformational executive education programs. *Academy of Management Learning and Education, 6*(3), 375–387.

Dreher, G. F., Dougherty, T. W., & Whitely, B. (1985). Generalizability of MBA degree and socioeconomic effects on business school graduates' salaries. *Journal of Applied Psychology, 70*(4), 769–773.

Ghoshal, S., Arnzen, B., & Brownfield, S. (1992). A learning alliance between business and business schools: Executive education as a platform for partnership. *California Management Review, 35*(1), 50–67.

Hura, G. (2003). A new model for executive education. *Journal of Executive Education, 2*(2), Article 1.

Jacobson, D., Chapman, R., Ye, C., & Os, J. (2017). A project-based approach to executive education. *Decision Sciences Journal of Innovative Education, 15*(1), 42–61.

Petit, F. (2011). Rethinking executive MBA programs. *MIT Sloan Management Review, 53*(1), 19–20.

Trieschmann, J. S., Dennis, A. R., Northcraft, G. B., & Nieme, A. W. (2000). Serving constituencies in business schools: MBA program versus research performance. *Academy of Management Journal, 43*(6), 1130–1141.

Ye, C., Van Os, J., Chapman, D., & Jacobson, D. (2017). An online project-based competency education approach to marketing education. *Journal of Marketing Education*, 10.1177.

Chapter 4

Business School Revenue Orientation

Introduction

At the core of every business school is a dialectic between two distinct aims − producing knowledge and educating students. On one hand there are research-intensive institutions and on the other are teaching-led, or even research-less, schools. Most schools are somewhere in between, leaving them with a dual system of purposes and corresponding metrics that are all too often contradictory and confusing rather than complementary and cohesive.

Every institution has a different strategic view and attacks different market segments with a range of alternative approaches (Antunes & Thomas, 2007; Fragueiro & Thomas, 2011; Iniguez de Onzono, 2011; Ivory, Miskell, & Shipton, 2006; Thomas, 2007). The choices that individual institutions make about their business models, value chains, and programme strategies broadly share one common element: financial volatility. A significant number of existing business schools appear to be financially unstable and probably unsustainable in the long run (Schlegelmilch & Thomas, 2011).

This chapter therefore seeks to explore business school strategy and choice. It explores the financial drivers of business schools on both the income and expenditure sides of the equation and highlights areas of distinct concern. On the basis of these analyses, it also offers some thoughts on how business educators can orient their future strategies and positioning to become more sustainable.

Sources of Revenue

Though not all schools are dependent on government funding many more rely on some form of direct or indirect financial support than are willing to admit in their statements of strategic intent and positioning (Ivory et al., 2006). State funding means that business schools are directly funded to educate students and, additionally, to produce research. Education is seen as a public good that produces an educated workforce, which in turn generates returns to a nation through higher productivity and taxes. Research generates innovation that also creates long-term public benefit.

While this traditional mode of funding is still strongly represented in continental Europe, it is increasingly being questioned on philosophical and financial grounds. In many nations, especially in Asia and Latin America, education is viewed generally as a private rather than a public benefit and funding is being adjusted accordingly.

It is clear that this view serves governments' purpose of reducing education funding in the face of intense competition for financial resources. Consequently, direct grants for education are being reduced and students are increasingly responsible for funding their own education, leading them increasingly to position their concerns about education quality from a strong "customer-oriented" perspective (Fethke & Policano, 2012). Direct grants have thus, via loans, become indirect grants to students.

In the UK, this process has been underway for some time. In the UK, while education was free to the user until 1997, fees have been increasing ever since. In 1998, annual undergraduate fees of £1,000 were introduced. This increased to £3,000 in 2004 and rose to £9,000 at a majority of institutions in 2012. Graduates are required to repay their loans over a lengthy period once they reach an annual income level above £21,000. The government has publicly stated that two-thirds of students would repay their loans. Privately, it agrees with the university sector, which expects only about one-third to repay. The truth will eventually become clear but perhaps not for as long as 30 years. Ironically, if eventual total repayments are less than 50% of the loans given out, the new system will prove to be more expensive than the one it replaced.

Reliance on government is also the key driver where one would least expect to find it: in the American for-profit educational sector populated by a wide range of providers. The vast majority of US students use Title IV federal loans to pay for their academic programmes. For-profits are actually the largest users of federal funding. Without this funding, which is presently being challenged in Congress because of poor completion rates of between 10% and 15% of students in some cases, the business model of the for-profits will certainly be less attractive in the future. The share prices of these providers are certainly signalling that expectation.

Underlying these Anglo-American examples is the question of what proportion of a given society ought to attend university. There are again two different modern models. The Anglo-American model seeks broad participation. Approximately 50% of all secondary school graduates continue on to university. In the Humboldt university model, which is common in continental Europe, universities aim for a narrower intellectual elite in the range of 20% of high-school graduates. In countries using the Humboldt model, financing universities is obviously less onerous.

In middle-income and developing countries, university attendance rates are more aligned with the Humboldt model, averaging, according to UNESCO (2007), a UN agency, around 20%. The role of government funding is also more modest than in the west. Public funding accounts for 54% of university budgets whereas in the richer OECD countries, approximately 76% of university funding originates from government (OECD, 2010).

If governments are unwilling to pay, then the burden falls on the user of services. This leads ultimately to the issue of whether the students, businesses, or parents are "Willing-to-Pay" the price of tuition. Yet because of the imbalance between demand and supply, fees have increased rapidly. The cost of MBA tuition in Western Europe in the 1990s rarely surpassed €10,000 while two decades later fees of €60,000 for full-time programmes are not uncommon with some EMBA programmes now having price tags of over €100,000.

In some cases, differentiation is also possible based on domestic versus non-domestic students. Presently, the annual fee for undergraduate education in the UK, for domestic and EU students, is £9,000 a year. Non-EU students pay on average £13,000. Similar ratcheting is common across the world. What will happen following Brexit, as the UK leaves the EU, is open for speculation as far as tuition fees go but one would expect EU students to face higher fees sooner or later.

Tuition in the US has reached extremely high levels. In 2011, more than 100 institutions charged over $50,000 a year for fees, room and board even at undergraduate level (Brown, 2011). By 2016, the combined figure for fees and tuition was well over $60,000. On this basis and extrapolating from present trends, fees for four-year undergraduate degree programmes in the US are likely to reach $330,000 by 2020 (Taylor, 2010). The top 20 MBA programmes in the US all ask tuition fees of around $120,000, which comes to about $170,000 if other costs are included while EMBA programmes cost up to $187,290 (Byrne, 2011).

Although historically students may have thought that the return on this investment was not unreasonable, the increasing costs of tuition and living expenses combined with potential loss of income during the programme may well lead to numerous candidates concluding that a tipping point and willingness to pay will soon be reached where the costs outweigh the benefits.

Other Sources of Funding

With government funding decreasing, business schools have turned to two more sources of funding: executive education and fundraising. Both can be tremendously lucrative but are not necessarily easy to establish nor guaranteed to be successful. As indicated in Chapter 3, business school value chains in executive education require a different infrastructure and faculty composition than that of degree programmes. And even when established, executive education is very volatile and hyper-competitive as illustrated by the impact of the last recession. Revenues reduced significantly within a matter of months. Unicon, a consortium of schools involved in executive education, reported that, on average, revenues generated by executive education have been under pressure and the current evidence suggest that the profitability of executive education has declined with the increased level of competition in the field (Eiter, Stine, & Woll, 2017).

Fundraising is the other potentially large source of external funding and proud and satisfied alumni and friends of schools can be very generous. Certainly the endowments of the world's top 10 universities are measured in billions rather than millions of euros. However, expectations about amounts likely be generated by the endowments have had to be amended recently as endowments have shrunk in real terms, as have the returns. Whereas in many cases such endowments might have accounted for up to 20% of funding, this is no longer the case. Furthermore, the number of universities where fundraising makes a substantial impact on operating budgets is actually very small and often the major impact is on the leading US universities.

Value-Based Strategic Orientation

As the price of education continues to rise for students and their benefactors, additional questions are raised regarding the value of the education and degree. As Brandenburger and Stuart Jr. (1996) note, the added value of a firm will find an upper bound based on market conditions and the customer's "willingness-to-pay". How much are students and their parents (or employers) willing to pay for business school programmes and degrees? While fees continue to rise, business school leaders must continue to ask this question in light of each programme – from undergraduate, postgraduate, through to executive education. The "Willingness-to-pay" is the most that students or other customers will pay for a business school programme. Competitive advantage for a given business school relative to another business school occurs when the value spread between willingness to sell (i.e. the lowest point at which a school can offer a programme) and the willingness to pay as defined above is larger.

The value-chain analysis presented in Chapters 2 and 3 suggests that there is both the buyer pressure on programme prices and cost pressure on the development and presentation of the various business school programmes. Rather than blindly setting prices based on market trends, business schools should proactively seek to understand the market pressures and alternatives to determine the perceived value of programmes and the willingness to pay of each type of customer. An orientation towards value creation by programme type along with a review of the value chain could help align the willingness to pay with programme features and offerings. Business school competition is expected to increase in many locations around the world and a clear value orientation and value capture strategy will be critical as the market changes.

Research vs. Teaching; Rigour vs. Relevance

In recent debates about higher education, one subject that has received only limited attention is surely the model by which business schools and universities manage their main strategic assets: their faculty. In most academic institutions, overall staffing costs, including faculty, can easily approach 75% of institutional expenditures.

These faculty members have priorities: teaching and research, which are often in conflict. In research-intensive universities as well as in many research-focused business schools, faculty members' career paths are dependent on their research productivity, measured by the number of publications in high quality research journals. The metrics are clear and are, unsurprisingly, output measures.

Input measures do not exist on the research front. How long does it take to write a paper? For some, a lifetime; for others, a weekend. Some individuals are able to develop collaborative infrastructures that include colleagues, graduate students and research assistants and as a result are able to generate many papers a year. The point here is a simple one: how much time should be devoted to research in contrast to other activities? How much and what types of research output should be expected?

In many cases research has become an end in itself as Bennis and O'Toole (2005), Pfeffer and Fong (2002, 2004), and Ghoshal (2005) have all pointed out. A special edition of the *British Journal of Management* (2011) questions the relevance of business school research. Many note that research reflects the fact that it is the academic departmental structures in universities as well as the "publish or perish" reward system that determines academic promotion rather than the interdisciplinary nature of business. This is genuinely unfortunate and is peculiar to business schools. In other professional schools such as medicine, architecture and engineering, research and practice are much more closely aligned. A fundamental rethink of the research model is required.

In some cases, research, whether journal-oriented or practice-based, is directly funded, financed by research grants from foundations or directly by government. But in most cases, research is cross-subsidised from teaching income. That is, premium-priced programmes such as EMBAs become the "cash cows" for funding a school.

Academics – Teaching and Revenue

The economics of teaching time is fascinating and peculiarly absent from the literature. While there are references to the "business school business model" in the literature: AACSB (2011), Iniguez de Onzono (2011), Ivory et al. (2006), the emphasis is on the income side not on the expenditure side. A core question regarding business school finances, surely, is what does an hour of teaching time cost and what does an hour of teaching time generate as revenue? These core calculations can then be scaled up to an annual calculation and be compared across the higher educational landscape with related knowledge-intensive businesses.

There are three research models in higher education. The first, a research-only model, will of necessity be left aside except as a cost to an institution that must be somehow borne. The second is a teaching-intensive model. In many teaching-based universities in the UK and elsewhere, there is an anchor at about 300 teaching hours a year per faculty member. Assuming a base faculty salary of $80,000 with typical on-costs for pensions, support staff and so on, one can model on the basis of a fully loaded cost of something in the region of $100,000 per faculty member. The teaching cost is thus about $333/hour.

At the research-intensive end of the spectrum, fully loaded salaries can be double that. The main factor, however, is the reduced teaching load. At 150 teaching hours per research faculty a year (120 for some universities), the hourly teaching cost is about $1,133. Within a similar calculation model, there are schools where average fully loaded salaries approach $300,000 with similarly low teaching loads. This leads to an hourly teaching cost of $2,500. No doubt someone somewhere is even more expensive on an hourly basis.

By comparison, secondary school teachers in middle-income and developing economies cost, on average, $10 per hour and in the OECD around $90 per hour (OECD, 2011). Consulting firms, referenced by Fragueiro and Thomas (2011) as an example for business schools without delving into their actual financing models, have a similarly bullish approach to costs per hour. Given that consultants can easily have a target of generating 200 billable days per year or an annual target of 1,600 billable hours, one will be looking at an hourly cost of something in the region of $94 per hour for a mid-level consultant.

While secondary school teachers and university teachers often fall into the realm of public servants, consultants are expected to generate three to three-and-a-half times their fully loaded costs per year. How does this work out in higher education? Perhaps more importantly, what should the level be given that there are probably many more non-income generating individuals in a university proportionally than in a for-profit consulting environment? The contrast is quite striking when comparing the cost per contact hour as shown in Table 4.1.

On an annually aggregated level, one of the authors' own institutions has calculated that individual faculty members generate between two-and-a-half and four times their fully loaded salaries. Anecdotally, a US colleague recently calculated that at his university, business school faculty generate on average $895, 000 per academic while colleagues at the school of fine arts generate only $210,000 per academic. Again, the non-academic cost base is key but at the lower end of both of these examples the economics of higher education seem less than ideal.

Given the economic infrastructure in place in higher education, there are two ways in which teaching costs can be managed. The first is what seems to be the trend: simply teach the students less. At undergraduate levels, contact time can appear rather thin: six to 10 hours of contact per week for 30 weeks a year is not unusual. A second lever is simply to

Table 4.1. Cost per Contact (Teaching) Hour.

Institution Type	Role	Annual Contact Hours	Annual Total Compensation	Cost per Contact Hour
Teaching-Based University	Lecturer	300	$100,000	$333
Research-Based University	Assistant Professor	150	$170,000	$1,133
Elite University	Professor	120	$300,000	$2,500
OECD Country Secondary School	Teacher	1040	$90,000	$87
Consulting Firm	Consultant	1600	$150,000	$94

increase the number of students in the classroom to drive costs per student down. Perhaps there is another option that needs to be considered. Is it realistic for universities to continue to operate only with their present range of models and levers or is it ultimately necessary to consider the unthinkable - increasing teaching loads or coming up with an alternative teaching model across the sector?

Increasing teaching loads would have an immediate effect on the economics of education. An increase from a three-course to a four-course annual teaching load would generate tremendous capacity and drive down costs considerably. An even greater increase in teaching loads would obviously generate even further efficiencies. Would this completely undermine a faculty member's ability to produce research or are we collectively simply unwilling to consider this as a partial solution to the challenges business education faces?

More radical would be to make official something that already happens surreptitiously at many institutions: the creation of a clinical faculty track that parallels the research and tenure faculty track. A dispassionate assessment of course content is illuminating. There is effectively a common body of knowledge that is diffused across many schools. Common case studies are used and text books change little across programmes in different schools. Van Hoek and Peters (2008) surveyed 166 supply chain academics who reported that only 10% to 15% of the material they used in their MBA courses was based on their own research. This raises the obvious question: what is our value proposition? Is it about the distinctive content created through our exploratory research and proprietary knowledge base or is it well-regarded programmes taught in a high quality and relevant manner?

Clinical faculty can surely be valuable if such a common body of knowledge also exists in other subject areas. Additionally, if clinical faculty were managed appropriately, students would benefit from more applied experience from industry and the school would benefit through higher teaching loads. An eight-course teaching load is surely feasible if one is focused on teaching and not on getting articles into top-tier academic journals. As noted earlier, secondary school teachers, while not strictly comparable, seem to manage.

Even more radical would be to consider the use of educational technologies. While not all management education is suited to online delivery, large parts surely are. Generic, input-driven bodies of knowledge that need to be learned can be delivered more efficiently through a thoughtful investment in e-learning than through expensive individual instructors. Surely it is also more interesting for faculty members to engage with the more advanced areas of their subjects than simply to begin at the beginning over and over again.

The Income Side of Teaching by Programme Type

Another perspective on the economics of business schools that is worth pursuing is to analyse the different values of the different activities: undergraduate, postgraduate and executive education as outlined in Chapters 2 and 3. Tuition and other income streams have already been covered in the round but not in detail. The value chain sections in Chapters 2 and 3 drew distinctions between undergraduate, pre-experience master's, MBAs, EMBAs, open executive programmes, custom learning and development programmes, and organisation development programmes. The same pattern follows here.

Tuition fees for undergraduate programmes vary considerably and involve both direct tuition income as well as grants directly to the university. Using the UK as an example, students who are UK and EU citizens pay £9,000 a year. For this, they get – in the example cited above – about 300 hours of teaching a year. While there are, of course, many other activities, ranging from preparation through to seminars and on to grading, we will ignore these for the moment. Each hour in the classroom thus brings in £30 per student. The multiplier effect is obviously the class size. With 40 students in the room, each hour brings in £1,200 per hour. With 80 students, the number becomes £2,400 per hour.

The same exercise conducted for US schools with tuition of approximately $45,000 and an assumption of a similar teaching schedule of 300 hours equates to $150 an hour per student. Scaled to 40 students, we arrive at $6,000 per hour; at 80 at $12,000 per hour. It should also be noted that the average cost of UK universities for international (non-UK and non-EU citizens) students is roughly comparable to the US cost model.

Carrying on with our income thinking exercise to pre-experience master's degrees, the same caveats apply. But for the sake of argument, let us pick £15,000 for UK calculations, and assume the same fees for Master's degrees as for undergraduate degrees per year in the US. The tricky bit here is the calculation of how much students are taught on the two sides of the Atlantic that we are using for our calculations. In business education, a master's degree tends to come in at approximately 500 teaching hours overall. In the UK, as well as in much of Europe, master's programmes tend to be approximately one year long. In North America, they tend to be two years. Thus, in the UK, assuming an average tuition of £15,000 and 500 taught hours, the per hour income per student is also £30 as with undergraduates. Scaling is the same with 40 students generating £1,200 per hour and 80 students generating £2,400.

In the US example, where the 500 hours are spread across two years, students are only getting 300 hours per year. At tuition of $50,000 per year, each hour generates $167 per student. At 40 students, that would be $6,667 per hour. At 80 students, this number would rise to $13,333 per hour as shown in Table 4.2.

We will explore the EMBA level to show the variance. We know that the top tuition fee is now about $180,000. We will, for the benefit of the doubt, allow for 500 overall teaching hours and assume a bursting classroom of 80 students. The calculations lead to breath-taking income streams per taught hour and day. Students are paying $360 per taught hour and are hopefully learning something while their bank accounts or, in all likelihood, the bank accounts of their employers are being rapidly depleted. With a classroom of 80 students, our conceptual business school is raking in $28,000 per hour. Given that many EMBA programmes are taught on a block-release basis and students can actually be in the classroom for eight-hour stretches, this would amount to $230,400 in one day of class!

A final thought here is that while pre-experience master's and MBA programmes often break class sizes down from core classes to electives

Table 4.2. Programme Revenue by Teaching Hour.

Programme Type	Fees/Year per Student	Teaching Hours/Year per Student	Fees/Hour per Student	Class of 40 Students	Class of 80 Students
UK Undergraduate	£9,000.00	300	£30.00	£1,200.00	£2,400.00
UK Graduate	£15,000.00	500	£30.00	£1,200.00	£2,400.00
USA Undergraduate	$45,000.00	300	$150.00	$6,000.00	$12,000.00
USA Graduate	$50,000.00	300	$166.67	$6,666.67	$13,333.33
USA EMBA	$180,000.00	500	$360.00	$14,400.00	$28,800.00
Executive Education	$1500/day	6/day	$250.00	$10,000.00	$20,000.00

and some EMBA programmes feature electives, others do not. Thus for a business school with a cohort being taught at the rates and assumptions described above it is like winning the lottery.

In a similar, vein, investigating the economics of open, custom and OD executive education activities is illustrative and perhaps counterintuitive. The most lucrative activity in the executive education realm is clearly a successful portfolio of open programmes.

In the UK and the US, programmes tend to charge between £1,000 and £1,500 per participant day with, surprisingly, considerable variance within this range even within individual institutions. Generally, the programmes operate on a six-hour teaching day to allow time for coffee breaks, lunch breaks and networking time. Daily income is simply the *per diem* cost multiplied by the number of attendees. Forty participants at £1,500 yield £60,000 on a daily basis or £10,000 an hour. Eighty participants on a large group programme priced at £1,500 *per diem* generate £20,000 per hour or £120,000 a day.

As an historical aside, custom programmes arose in many cases from an individual organisation's desired to have content tailored to its own needs but also because, surprising as it may seem, learning and development purchasers can also do their calculations. Beginning in the mid-1980s, demand for custom programmes began to surpass demand for open programmes in many institutions.

Programmes vary widely in pricing, and getting detailed figures is notoriously difficult. Schools, much like individual faculty members, tend to quote what they would like to get or the most they were ever paid for a teaching day rather than how much they will actually work for. From our experience, pricing also has two components − days for preparation and days of teaching. For the former, preparation *per diems* tend to follow consulting pricing and will fall into the region of £3,000 to £4,000 per faculty day. Delivery, which is often done using two faculty members per day, gets billed in a range between £12,000 and £25,000 leading to a per faculty member a day income stream of £6,000 to £12,500.

Custom OD intervention sales processes, as we noted earlier in the chapter on executive education value chains, do feature business schools but they will compete with consultants and OD boutiques. The pricing model is thus based not on delivery days as such but on days worked. Rates here are much lower than for custom interventions, certainly when the clients are in the public sector. Rates below £2,000 *per diem* are certainly not uncommon.

While not all business schools face financial challenges in the near term, fault lines are clearly visible. Traditional sources of income are less stable than they used to be. Government, the primary source of funding in OECD countries, will not expand educational budgets continually. Student tuition cannot go on rising forever. At many MBA programmes tuition has reached levels that are not sustainable and pose real questions of value and fairness.

As noted above, income from executive education is not the "golden goose" it is held up to be. This may perhaps not hold for schools that can run large cohorts on their open programmes, though custom programmes are not as lucrative as often imagined.

On the cost side, many institutions are using a faculty model that is very luxurious. No other industries that we can think of use their main human capital to directly generate income for less than 10% of their annual time at the low end of the spectrum and only about 30% at the highest.

Revenue Delivered View (RDV) — Towards a Common Currency in Teaching

In research-oriented business schools, faculty view teaching as an obligation. It is a well-understood model that is not unique to business schools and permeates the halls of higher education as faculty are generally rewarded for their research and publications rather than teaching though, of course, teaching is an important part of the role of faculty and high teaching scores are often considered relevant in faculty hiring, appraisals and promotions.

It should be noted that the orientation towards research varies significantly based on the individual institution and the emphasis of the current administration. The expectations for different types of faculty may also vary. For example, faculty hired for the primary role of teaching (lecturers, practice-based) will be evaluated more directly on teaching scores and track records while tenure-track or research-based faculty will be evaluated more on their publications and citations generated.

As one research faculty who was up for tenure review comments: "As long as my teaching is around the average, I should be okay... If my teaching scores are too high or if I am doing extra teaching then the review committee may not think that I am a serious researcher!"

A contributing factor to this de-emphasis on teaching is the "common currency" factor of value creation through research. What we mean by "common currency" is that the success of a research faculty member is very transparent and universally recognised. While each business school may attribute value in different ways, there is a rather scientific approach to counting citations, the impact factor of leading journals and the number of publications. This creates a common way of valuing research and scholarly contributions across institutions. In other words, the value of one's research is recognised by the academic population. However, the evaluation of teaching relies on school-specific measures and is subject to geographical nuances that are not generally transferable.

The evaluation of teaching effectiveness is a hotly debated topic. It has long been recognised that student evaluations of teaching are fraught with biases and false indicators of learning (Clayson, 2008). However, most schools continue to rely on student feedback as a primary indicator of instructor quality since it is relatively easy to measure and administer. This institution-specific orientation to teaching effectiveness along with a lack of transparency can lessen the perceived importance of this measure. While all faculty members generally want to do well in teaching, most recognise that the effort to be a popular and well-liked professor with students is not consistent with their orientation towards sharing knowledge and creating a challenging learning environment. And yes, this can be a bit disheartening to parents who are struggling to pay the hefty tuition bills for business school education!

In considering the revenue sources of a business school, the research vs teaching orientation creates a potential discontinuity of priorities. While good research can create increased recognition along with research rankings, it is not so well-aligned with the paying customer. Of course, good research can create improved revenue via grants but not nearly to the same extent as tuition revenue. This discontinuity between faculty operations and revenue is further exacerbated by business school rankings (Khurana, 2007).

Rankings are largely centred on the success of programmes and their teaching. But as prices for business education continue to rise, there are a growing number of questions about the effectiveness and uniqueness of business school teaching.

Could we develop a common currency for teaching that is aligned to the revenue-generation of a school? Consider how professional services firms work with clients and align the measures of their staff towards common goals. Mintzberg (2004) provided a perspective on business schools as professional organisations in his review of McGill University.

Fragueiro and Thomas (2011) provide a comparison of business schools and professional services firms in their work on strategic leadership in a business school. Whether one can run a business school like a services firm is a debated topic though Fragueiro and Thomas show a strong similarity in terms of the demands on business school leaders.

In a professional services firm there is the challenge of managing individual professionals and providing ways to align the organisation. At senior levels of a law firm, search firm or consulting firm, the partners are generally evaluated on sales, revenue delivered and staff satisfaction. Each of these components can have various measures (contracted engagements, billable hours, client satisfaction and staff turnover) but are generally in line with the profitability and growth of a firm.

Business schools, thankfully, do not involve faculty in the sales process (one can only imagine the folly of asking a quantitative finance professor to convince potential MBA students to join a course) but do rely on faculty for the delivery of revenue (teaching). Just as in a professional services firm, faculty members have varying degrees of competence in teaching across programme types and levels. In professional services firms, staff are recognised for their ability to deliver a wider and more complex array of client engagements. In most business schools, the orientation to revenue delivered or programme challenge is largely ignored.

It is not uncommon for a business school faculty member to teach five sections of an undergraduate course to satisfy his or her teaching requirement while other faculty members may teach one EMBA course, one master's course, one MBA course and two different undergraduate electives. While the value of each contribution is quite different in terms of both utility as well as difficulty (expectations of EMBA students are quite high as covered in Chapter 3), most business schools would acknowledge these as equal contributions. This further decreases incentives for faculty to take on more challenging teaching assignments.

To calculate revenue delivered by course module, one multiplies the fees/hour per student by the standard teaching hours per course module (we assume 30 hours in most universities). So an MBA programme would generate $4,980 per student per course module. If there were 70 students in the course module, then the instructor would be delivering $348,600 in revenue. The same can be done with other programme types as shown in Table 4.3.

While this analysis will vary by school, it begins to highlight some critical differences in terms of revenue delivered. For the tuition cost, we use the entire programme duration (bachelor's degree may be over

Table 4.3. Revenue Delivered by Program Type.

Program Type	Fees/ Hour per Student	Teaching Hours per Course Module	Course Module Revenue per Student	Average Number of Students	Revenue Delivered per Course Module
Undergraduate	$150	30	$4,500	60	$270,000
Master's	$150	30	$4,500	80	$360,000
MBA	$166	30	$4,980	70	$348,600
EMBA	$370	30	$11,100	50	$555,000
Exec Ed	$250	12	$3,000	50	$150,000

four years while an executive education course may be two days) and consider only the number of required course modules not all the courses offered. Of course, the number of students in courses may vary widely, with some undergraduate courses involving 200 first-year students while upper-class electives may have only 20 students. There are ways to adjust for these situations but we will keep the model simple for now.

Taking the above example of programme types along with the hypothetical revenue, one can begin to see how we might view the revenue delivered contribution of different faculty members (Table 4.4). The stylised model of a potential business school is assumed in this case and populated with three hypothetical faculty members we shall call Professors X, Y and Z. For this example, Professor X teaches primarily undergraduate courses, Professor Y teaches at all levels and across programmes and Professor Z teaches at the postgraduate and executive levels.

Let us assume the Professor X teaches five undergraduate courses with an average of 60 students in each section. He also teaches one executive education course with 50 students. Using the course revenue per student, one can calculate that his total revenue delivered contribution is $1.5 million. We can contrast that to Professor Y, who teaches across all programmes as well as executive education, with a total of more than $2 million delivered. Professor Z also teaches five sections in two programmes but she also teaches five days of executive education to deliver more than $2.5 million to the school.

In most business schools, the difference in value delivered by programme is not recognised, with the exception of executive education.

Table 4.4. Revenue Delivered by Faculty.

Examples	Undergrad	Master's	MBA	EMBA	Exec Ed	Total Revenue Delivered
Prof X Course Sections	5	0	0	0	1	
Prof X #Students	300	0	0	0	50	
Prof X Revenue Delivered	$1,350,000	$0	$0	$0	$150,000	**$1,500,000**
Prof Y Course Sections	2	1	1	1	2	
Prof Y #Students	100	80	70	50	100	
Prof Y Revenue Delivered	$450,000	$360,000	$348,600	$555,000	$300,000	**$2,013,600**
Prof Z Course Sections	0	3	2	0	5	
Prof Z #Students	0	240	140	0	250	
Prof Z Revenue Delivered	$0	$1,080,000	$697,200	$0	$750,000	**$2,527,200**

Due to the short nature of these programmes, they are generally not counted toward teaching load requirements and faculty members are given a stipend for each day of teaching. While some might argue that executive education should not be included in our analysis, we recognise that the revenue from executive education programmes is often critical to the operating budget of a school. After all, our goal is to consider how we might align faculty teaching with school revenue.

This type of analysis would also allow us to highlight stronger teachers who have more students sign up for their courses. If Prof Q and Prof R both teach five undergraduate courses but Prof Q has a better reputation for teaching, then she will naturally have more students. As one experienced professor once remarked: "The better you are with teaching, the more the students want to sign up for your courses... so you are punished with more work for doing well."

A Composite Measure: Teaching Quality vs. Revenue Delivered

Highlighting revenue delivered may help us to not only consider the relative contribution of faculty towards the goals of a school but also allow us to take a step towards a "common currency" as we consider hiring and promotion decisions.

One potential drawback of this orientation to revenue is that faculty may become overly focused on a revenue number and this will lead to difficult salary discussions and will diminish the importance of research. While salary issues will always be present in academia, this type of orientation might actually help highlight to school administrations how to better allocate scarce funding and support. It may also reveal salary discrepancies between research-oriented faculty and teaching faculty (though that can also be a good opportunity to further align contributions). The use of a measure like this is not to replace the focus on research measures but to balance the contribution to research with effectiveness in teaching.

Completing this analysis can be done easily; however, using this information for faculty measurement may create unintended consequences. What if faculty realise that they are only earning a small fraction of the revenue that they deliver? This is certainly true in professional services firms at all levels as employees are billed at rates that are several times their own salaries.

But while consultants may understand the business model and their role in making it work it is doubtful that most faculty have the clarity of understanding or line of sight on their own contribution to their institution.

Another concern with the focus on revenue is that faculty may work towards volume vs. quality of teaching. In other words, a faculty member may teach high-volume classes to achieve a higher level of revenue delivered though the quality may not be that strong. This is likely not sustainable in executive education or in master programmes but could be a shorter-term issue. One way to address this is to factor the teaching evaluation scores with the revenue delivered model.

Taking our sample faculty members (Prof X, Prof Y and Prof Z). Let us assume that the overall teaching evaluations are scored on a scale of 1-7 (with seven as a high mark). Their scores are 5.75, 4.9 and 6.4 respectively. Let us assume that the teaching scores are calibrated across programme types to arrive at an average for the instructor for the year. We can then plot the teaching scores with the revenue generated by faculty member. The teaching composite profile is shown in Figure 4.1.

In this case, we see that Prof Y delivers significant revenue but not at a satisfactory level for teaching evaluations. Viewing this with two measures can help calibrate expectations just as we expect with research (multiple publications vs impact rating of journals). In most consulting firms, this calibration is done when considering revenue delivered and client satisfaction.

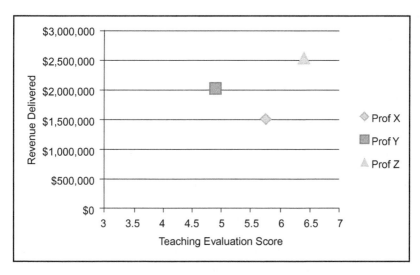

Figure 4.1.   Teaching Composite Profile.

Other concerns with this type of orientation might include the overly managerial orientation of a business school culture. After all, we are not running a consulting firm or a law firm. However, it may be time to align business schools more aptly to a professional school orientation such as we see in law and medicine. While this certainly may be a concern with educators around the world, the business of business schools has become, as we have stated have throughout this book – business.

One of the fundamental challenges facing institutions is how to reconcile traditional research expectations with the profit-driven orientation of business schools. By taking a view on revenue delivered, we might help create some level of alignment between faculty and administration.

While this type of measure may raise eyebrows in many hallowed hallways, the shifting nature of business schools requires a different orientation towards teaching. We have a common currency to evaluate and acknowledge the contributions of academics as we track citations, publications and impact. Perhaps it is time we had a common currency that is aligned to our primary source of revenue – teaching others. Imagine seeing faculty CVs that list publications and citations along with revenue delivered and teaching scores. We then might have a full picture of the contribution and value of our faculty members in line with the goals of our institutions.

Summary and Conclusions

There are actions that business schools can take to address many of the challenges outlined above. The question is whether they are willing to do so as individual institutions or whether the "system" of business education will get in the way – in other words, other schools will not change their systems and so systemically nothing changes.

The income side is hard to shift. Schools can, however, seek to diversify their streams of income into adjacent fields such as executive education, work-based learning and online learning. There are already UK-based universities that have gone further and are involved in housing, transport and entertainment industry offerings.

The cost side offers greater possibilities. Instead of endlessly bemoaning the lack of academically (doctoral) qualified faculty, business schools should realistically introduce a parallel track of clinical faculty who have higher teaching loads but are also required to be up-to-date on industry developments. Clinical or practice-based faculty would additionally publish and make impact in both high quality applied journals but not necessarily contribute to the citations in top-tier academic journals.

By investing in learning technologies, business schools can provide valuable, cost-effective tuition in many of the basic areas of management. This will then allow an efficient, high value-added use of faculty time as they will be able to focus on more sophisticated, complex areas of the business curriculum. Business school academics need also to be realistic about their own teaching loads. By accepting to teach one additional class, major benefits can accrue to their institutions and, by extension, to their own working environment.

More broadly, business school associations and accrediting agencies, as well as media organisations that rank business schools, ought also to reflect on the expectations they have of business schools.

A variety of alternative examples of business schools presently exist. Many are outside the mainstream, such as the predominantly adjunct-based models of some of the for-profit business schools. Others are trying to change the system from within (Fraguiero & Thomas, 2011; Lorange, 2008). By acknowledging the equal roles of clinical and research faculty, by abolishing tenure and introducing performance-related pay or by emphasising teaching performance rather than research output as the primary form of evaluation, the dynamics and economics of business education can be changed. These alternatives, however, remain isolated examples rather than general trends.

All of these challenges are taking place in a rapidly changing educational landscape. These include the role of for-profits, the welcome growth of middle-income and developing countries' own educational infrastructure, and the advent of recessions and cost pressures in the competitive environment. More broadly, they are taking place in a world where uncertainty is very high and, critically, where genuine thought must be given to climate change, resource constraints, ever-increasing populations and sustainability.

Business schools are surely in a position to give real thought on what type of business model is appropriate for business when it seems obvious that continuing to expand consumption is not feasible, that financial short-termism is dangerous and that stewardship, reflecting corporate social responsibility and sustainability as opposed to maximising shareholder value, is surely what it needed. We thus believe it is time for a serious reflection on the sustainability and purpose of business education and a closer examination of how successful professional schools elsewhere (law, medicine, engineering) have created legitimate business models that have allowed them to prosper.

References

AACSB International. (2011). *Globalization of management education: Changing international structures, adaptive strategies and the impact on institutions. (Report of the AACSB International Globalization of Management Education Task Force)*. Bingley, UK: Emerald Group Publishing Limited.

Antunes, D., & Thomas, H. (2007). The Competitive (dis)advantages of European business schools. *Long Range Planning, Elsevier, 40*(3), 382−404.

Bennis, W. G., & O'Toole, J. (May 2005). How business schools lost their way. *Harvard Business Review, 83*(5), 96−104, 154.

Brandenburger, A. M., & Stuart, H. W., Jr. (1996). Value-based business strategy. *Journal of Economics & Management Strategy, 5*(1), 5−24.

Brown, R. (2011). Lessons from America. *Higher Education Policy Institute.* Retrieved from http://www.hepi.ac.uk

Byrne, J. (2011). The world's most expensive MBA program. Available at www.poetsandquants.com

Clayson, D. E. (2008). Student evaluations of teaching: Are they related to what students learn? *Journal of Marketing Education, 31*(1), 16−30.

Eiter, M., Stine, J., & Woll, T. (2017). Changing organizational models of executive education: Exploring beyond traditional boundaries. *Unicon Executive Education Research Report.* Retrieved from https://www.uniconexed.org/unicon-research-report-february-2017/

Fethke, G., & Policano, A. (2012). *Public no more: A new path to excellence for America's public universities.* Stanford, CA: Stanford University Press.

Fragueiro, F., & Thomas, H. (2011). *Strategic leadership in the business school: Keeping one step ahead.* Cambridge: Cambridge University Press.

Ghoshal, S. (2005). Bad management theories are destroying good management practices. *Academy of Management Learning & Education, 4*(1), 75−91.

Iniguez de Onzono, S. (2011). *The learning curve: How business schools are re-inventing education.* Basingstoke, UK: Palgrave McMillan.

Ivory, C., Miskell, P., & Shipton, H. (2006). *UK business schools: Historical contexts and future scenarios (Rep.).* Retrieved from https://www.bl.uk/collection-items/uk-business-schools-historical-contexts-and-future-scenarios

Khurana, R. (2007). *From higher aims to hired hands: The social transformation of American business schools and the unfulfilled promise of management as a profession.* Princeton, NJ: Princeton University Press.

Lorange, P. (2008). *Thought leadership meets business: How business schools can become more successful.* Cambridge, UK: Cambridge University Press.

Mintzberg, H. (2004). *Managers, not MBAs: A hard look at the soft practice of managing and management development.* Berrett-Koehler Publishers.

OECD. (2010). Tertiary graduation and entry rates. In *OECD factbook 2010: Economic, environmental and social statistics* (pp. 182−183). OECD Publishing.

OECD. (2011). Indicator D3: How much are teachers paid? In *Education at a glance 2011: OECD indicators* (pp. 406–421). OECD Publishing.

Pfeffer, J., & Fong, C. T. (2002). The end of business schools? Less success than meets the eye. *Academy of Management Learning & Education, 1*(1), 78–95.

Pfeffer, J., & Fong, C. T. (2004). The business school "Business": Some lessons from the US experience. *Journal of Management Studies, 41*(8), 1501–1520.

Schlegelmilch, B. B., & Thomas, H. (2011). The MBA in 2020: Will there still be one? *Journal of Management Development, 30*(5), 474–482.

Taylor, M. (2010). *Crisis on campus: A bold plan for reforming our colleges and universities.* Toronto: Knopf Doubleday Publishing.

Thomas, H. (2007). An analysis of the environment and competitive dynamics of management education. *Journal of Management Development, 26*(1), 9–21.

UNESCO. (2007). *Education counts: World education indicators.* Available at www.uis.unesco.org

Van Hoek, R. I., & Peters, B. K. G. (2008). Welk wetenschappelijk onderzoek bereikt de collegezaal? (Does research make it into the classroom and does it matter?). *Tijdschrift voor Hoger Onderwijs, 26*(3), 180–189.

Chapter 5

Value Proposition and Portfolio Choices

Introduction

The last chapter looked at the value chains associated with the various offerings from business schools and assessed the sources of revenues along with their strategic implications. This chapter considers the portfolio choices that institutions may need to address. Broad strategic groupings are suggested to put the choices into context and as a basis for considering strategy.

Examining the business model of today's business schools first requires consideration of the value propositions being provided. However, identifying a clear value proposition can be difficult given the multiple stakeholders and complexity of business schools as institutions. For example, the value proposition for a consumer retail business such as McDonalds can be identified as low-cost, family-friendly, fast food. From this value proposition, we could begin to think about alternative business models that might help address the challenges of operating physical restaurants. However, the value proposition and sets of customers are not always readily apparent in the case of a business school. As a start, consider the value proposition for universities in general.

The origins of the university concept can be traced to medieval times when groups of teachers and students would work together in pursuit of knowledge. Cardinal Newman's idea of the university (1852) was that it was a place for teaching universal knowledge including the arts, sciences and philosophy. The value proposition associated with these early universities was the development of scholarly expertise that would benefit society (Kerr, 2001). This benefit to society was further evaluated in the 1960s in the UK at a time when university education was spreading around the world. At that time, the benefit to society included instructing in sets of skills, the shaping of cultivated men and women, balancing research with teaching and transmitting common standards of citizenship (The Robbins Report, 1963).

While this value proposition can still be applied to universities today, the modern business school has taken a divergent path due to the emphasis on shareholder capitalism as noted in Chapter 1. Business schools have moved away from the idea of serving multiple stakeholders in society (Muff, 2012) to creating an entire industry of management education (Khurana, 2007; Pfeffer & Fong, 2002). The original, primarily vocational, concept behind the early business schools was the desire for professional managers who were qualified using an approach much like the training in medicine or law. As outlined in Chapters 2 and 3, there are two sometimes competing dimensions of business schools between the more traditional university orientation (the science of business) and the profit-making "industry" of management education as summarised in Table 5.1.

This management education industry is largely centred on the perceived monetary value of the MBA and executive education. The value proposition for customers of these programmes is straightforward. Business schools allbut promise that their graduates will have higher salaries, move ahead faster and be more successful. And, of course, the rankings game reinforces this rather transparent and capitalistic value proposition. Princeton University stands out as one of the few highly respected institutions that has not established a business school due to the perceived trade-offs between capitalistic intent and scholarly orientation.

To be fair, the other dimensions of a business school are more in line with the expectations of other university schools centred on research and undergraduate education. In an engineering school, for example, one would expect to find a strong focus on research, undergraduate teaching and postgraduate research. The same is true in most business

Table 5.1. Competing Business School Priorities.

	Science of Business	**Management Education**
Activity	Research, Undergraduate Teaching, Postgraduate Research	MBA, Exec Ed
Goals	Further the Profession, Share Knowledge	High Enrollment, High Ranking, High Satisfaction
Customer	Society	Managers/Firms
Value Proposition	Human Capital	Financial Success

schools when we remove the MBA and executive education programmes. However, even the academic orientation in business schools is now receiving significant criticism due to the focus on analytics and scientific rigour at the expense of wisdom (Mintzberg, 2004). While this is not unlike some criticisms of law and medical schools, business schools have not developed management as a profession (Pfeffer & Fong, 2004). Rather, the booming industry of management education has provoked much debate about the relevance of business school research and the orientation towards profit over knowledge.

As already discussed, it is precisely this profit-making opportunity via management education that changed the nature of business schools and now puts the future of many business schools in question. Any consideration of the future options for business schools must first recognise that not all business schools are the same (Thomas, Lorange, & Sheth, 2013). In addition to educational philosophy and approach, there are critical differences in the underlying business foundations between schools in how they operationalise their strategic choices across their value chains. While there is often a "follow the leader" tendency for schools to mimic what is done at the top-ranked schools, the strategic options as well as limitations will be quite different depending on the profile of the institution. So, rather than discussing strategic options with a broad brush, the following is an attempt to review the strategic considerations underlying a few more common models to help highlight contextual considerations for business school portfolios.

Managing and Strategising a Business School Portfolio

Every business school requires an understanding of the context and culture of the unique market in which it operates as well as knowledge of the capabilities of the institution and its faculty. Determining the type of portfolio and options involves many variations. For simplicity, we choose three scenarios: publicly funded, private institution and elite business school. Elite schools (consistent top-50 ranking) are separated because, typically, their significant brand equity and high demand for their programmes affords them more options.

In essence, these three scenarios comprise the broad categories of strategic groups of business schools across different countries and contexts. Below is a review of each type and consideration of their portfolio options and potential limitations. At the outset it should be noted that strategic groups are solely categorization devices. These groupings do not imply for example that all public schools or private schools achieve either the same levels of success or performance. Leaders and strategists within these schools will clearly attempt to differentiate their individual strategic approaches based on the location and resources available.

Publicly Funded Institutions

The most common and often most financially limited form of business school is the publicly funded school. Around the world, education has been an important priority at a national and local level as economists have shown the clear linkage between economic growth and human capital capability. Funding universities has been a key item in the economic growth and development of China and India as each nation has rapidly transformed its economy. In the west, the level of state funding has been strained, reduced and often questioned. In the US, many states are facing significant fiscal pressure due to other priorities such as an ageing population and crumbling infrastructure and are unable to continue to support education as in the past.

At the same time, university presidents are facing public challenges regarding the rising cost of tuition for undergraduate programmes. Several are even posing fundamental questions about the value of a college education (Cappelli, 2015) and the students' "willingness-to-pay" the rising tuition fees. This has been highlighted recently in the US where the cost of tuition in public universities has more than quadrupled over the past 30 years (though most of this is due to a reduction of state subsidies and shifting the burden to fall more on the student) (Campos, 2015).

But even in the face of increased costs the global demand for business education has been rising significantly, largely due to the rapid economic development of countries such as China, India and Brazil where millions of young people look to university to further their education and qualifications, leading to a larger percentage of the population in such countries attending universities.

This increase in demand for education, coupled with growing competition for top students, has fuelled additional university spending and put even greater focus on the student experience and marketing efforts. Fully-paying international students have become a great source of growth for many business schools and the publicly funded schools are no exception.

The temptation to fill the classrooms with international students paying full fees has caught the attention of public officials in a number of countries. In Singapore, for example, the Ministry of Education carefully monitors and caps the number of international undergraduate students to ensure educational opportunities exist for the citizens of the country. In North Carolina in the US, government officials have placed significant restrictions on the acceptance of international and out-of-state applicants to allow ample opportunities for state residents.

There are rationales all sides. One can argue that this attitude restricts publicly funded schools from attracting the best students from around the world (Brustein, 2007). Others suggest that authorities should seek a balance, obtaining a geographically diverse class with the value of creating an enriched experience for local students (Denson & Chang, 2009). The challenge for the publicly funded schools is managing consistent expectations with both local and global stakeholders. International (non EU) students will likely be paying 50% more than national students in Europe, and four or five times the amount their local counterparts pay in some Asian educational systems, yet all the services and experiences are standardised across the student population.

The demand from prospective students in Asia, Latin America, Eastern Europe and, more recently, Africa to attend programmes at western business schools has been a boon for such schools around the world over the last decade. But it is now starting to shift.

The rapid development of universities in China, India and other parts of the world plus declining numbers of students means more lecture room seats and fewer students to fill them. This reversal in demand will likely hit the publicly funded institutions first.

Why? Part of the reason is the way that undergraduate admissions operations typically filter applicants. It is common practice for university admissions to operate with "catchment zones" by state, country and/or region. An admissions department looks closely at its assigned catchment zones to find the best candidates in that zone – which is then balanced across all (global) applicants. In other words, a university may require a higher level of qualification for candidates from India relative to candidates from Russia to keep a desired balance of diversity in the classroom and the student population generally. While top schools will often attract top students, public institutions may be forced to alter their standards to continue the desired flow of international student applicants.

In addition to declining applications, publicly funded schools are often burdened with significant pension liabilities. State institutions are often required to offer retiree medical and pension programmes that face the strain of funding as baby-boomers retire (and then live longer). While other institutions may also face such challenges, the publicly funded institutions tend to be more closely governed and typically open to a more paternal approach to benefits and pensions. Imagine explaining to your students that the school will not revamp the study spaces in the library because they are too strapped paying retired faculty pensions.

Many governments provide tuition assistance to citizens or residents to help offset rising costs. This tuition assistance may be provided directly to the institution or provided to the students in the form of grants, loans or other aid. In the US, individual states contribute to higher education costs for residents. While state spending on education has increased over time, this has not kept pace with the rising number of students. Most states allocate between 5% and 16% of revenue to higher education but the contribution per student has been rapidly declining as college enrolments have increased over the last two decades.

Given these factors, the public university business school is facing a number of challenges. First, at the undergraduate level, many students are opting for education in the STEM domains (science, technology, engineering and maths). According to the US National Science Foundation (2016), the number of science and engineering degrees awarded has grown by more than 50% since 2000. To address this, many business schools are working to attract students with more practice-oriented curricula (internships, project-based learning, analytics labs) and application-based majors such as entrepreneurship, supply chain management, accounting and financial markets.

Second, the number of MBA and EMBA applicants is declining as the promise of a ROI on such an investment is called into question. This is especially true for most public universities. The number of people who are willing to spend up to two years in a full-time course of study has declined greatly. For most public business schools, the part-time or online MBA holds potential promise for the future. Third, the demand for executive education has declined in recent years with the increased availability of information and resources through online training or business consultants.

These challenges put increasing pressure on publicly funded business schools. A stylised revenue model for a public business school is shown in Table 5.2. This illustrates a high reliance on a large undergraduate student population alongside a relatively small set of graduate

Table 5.2. Example Revenue Sources for a Publicly Funded Business School.

Program	Students	Annual Tuition	State Funding	Total Revenue
Undergraduates	6000	$15,000	$10,000	$150,000,000
Master's	200	$40,000	$0	$8,000,000
MBA	120	$50,000	$0	$6,000,000
EMBA	50	$60,000	$0	$3,000,000
PhD	90	$10,000	$10,000	$1,800,000
Exec Ed	1000	$3,000	$0	$3,000,000
				$171,800,000

programmes such as the MBA and EMBA. While graduate programmes are a great source of revenue for elite institutions, offering traditional MBA programmes with limited scale is unlikely to be profitable once student services such as placement and marketing are taken into account.

Growing, or even maintaining, the revenue of a publicly funded business school is not an easy endeavour. The first priority is to secure and grow the undergraduate student population. This involves not only effort in attracting local students to the business school but also in working to expand an international reach. A strong undergraduate programme coupled with a PhD programme will provide a solid foundation for research-oriented faculty in a traditional university setting. As mentioned earlier, this fulfils the value proposition of creating human capital to serve the needs of society. While this solid foundation is sufficient for running a business school, it likely does not meet the aspirational goals of the institution to provide management education.

For the public university business school, management education in the form of MBAs and executive education is an attractive offering as an additional revenue stream with potentially high margins. However, it is often difficult to make these programmes successful in the traditional classroom model given the competition from private schools. Private, and certainly elite, business schools not only have ample demand for places in their programmes but also enjoy significantly better placement rates and salaries. To compete, publicly funded business schools typically offer their programmes at a significantly lower price and may need to invest more in the marketing of their programmes, thus eroding margins for many business schools. Yet most business schools feel a need to offer an MBA and executive education programmes to meet the needs of the local community.

Some schools may find that part-time MBA programmes allow more flexibility and may attract local working professionals, depending on the nature and size of the community.

However, is there a better way for publicly funded business schools to compete in the MBA market and other areas of management education?

New business models are starting to emerge as public universities work to further their reach and impact in management education. Online learning has become more popular in MBA programmes for public universities as this can eliminate the barrier of being physically present to attend classes. There is some evidence that public universities may become low-cost players in management education and strive for a significant volume of students.

The University of Illinois at Urbana-Champaign recently launched its iMBA programme, partnered with Coursera, a provider of massively open on-line courses (MOOCs). Under this programme, students can earn an MBA degree from the University of Illinois by taking free online courses for a significant portion of the study. Though it is a new programme it already has more than 800 students from 17 different countries enrolled. The total cost to students is currently at \$22,000 for the iMBA (if they choose to take exams to gain the MBA degree) while their traditional classroom-based MBA is estimated at \$57,000 a year for two years (assuming out-of-state tuition). This is an eye-opening example of a publicly funded business school making a big shift to capture an online space to grow its graduate business school. By partnering with distance learning platform providers, public universities can provide a new channel to market without significant investment. While critics might suggest that this may compromise the brand, the interest in reaching untapped markets can be appealing to school administrators.

The future strategy of the publicly funded business school seems to require a strong and vibrant undergraduate programme to continue to attract top-quality students. These schools will have a challenge in the broader management development space and will need to carefully consider their strategic portfolio choices in this area. It does seem that there is a market for new and aggressive business models involving distance learning at scale alongside relatively lower-cost programmes to compete globally with well-branded and respected private institutions.

It should be noted that some publicly funded business schools compare favourably with some of the private and elite schools. For example, the business schools at the University of California at both Berkeley and Los Angeles (UCLA), have done well with high demand for programmes due to their locations and strong performance over the years.

Private Institutions

Private universities tend to dominate the top of the business school rankings but these are generally also the elite schools. Since the elite schools compete differently and have varying strategic options they will be considered later as a separate strategic group.

Private universities come in a variety of forms. Several of the oldest university systems are private as are most of the new players in the industry. Private universities also have a higher failure rate as they may not have the size or ability to adapt to meet changing student needs. Thunderbird Global School of Management in the US declined as its MBA enrolments plummeted from over 1,000 students in 2001 to just over 100 students in 2014. With a declining endowment fund, Thunderbird was forced to find an acquisition partner in Arizona State University.

Though private institutions do not receive funding from government, they often benefit from tax incentives, non-profit status or other favourable treatment. Some private schools are supported by religious entities while others are entrepreneurial endeavours. Private business schools generally rely on full-paying students and typically focus more attention on the student experience and teaching. Private business schools can be big business as the growth of private universities around the world continues. Estimates show that over 30% of post-secondary education enrolment in the US is with private institutions (Levy, 2013).

Private business schools, especially the more established ones, actively manage alumni relations. Due to their generally smaller size, graduates of such schools may have more of a personal connection to their *alma mater* and feel more of a sense of obligation to support it (Baade & Sundberg, 1996). In 2014, universities in the US raised more than $37 billion dollars (Will, 2015). Alumni relations, involvement and donations generally feature quite prominently in private institutions that have an established alumni base. With more established private schools, there can also be legacy effects with generations of family members attending the same institution, which can also increase the potential for alumni giving. Research on donations from business school alumni shows a number of key factors including family ties, availability of gift matching, willingness to recommend the university to others and time since graduation (Okunade & Berl, 1997). Private business schools consistently do well with donations as alumni with high-ranking business titles give more, especially when they have maintained network ties with other alumni (Wunnava & Okunade, 2013).

While more established private business schools might have significant alumni donations and a healthy endowment fund (sometimes in the billions of dollars), many private schools struggle to meet their financial and growth targets.

In the developing economies of Asia, Africa and Latin America, private schools have helped meet the growing demand for business education. As developing countries move to market-based economies, they see a rapid increase in demand for business education (Kraft & Vodopoviec, 2003). In China, for example, the number of private universities grew from 20 in 1997 to over 600 by 2010 (Butrymowicz, 2012). Similar growth is now taking place in Africa where enrolment in higher education has grown by over 170% in the past 15 years according to the ICEF Monitor (2015). These numbers are expected to continue to grow as many developing countries strive to achieve higher-education enrolment rates.

In addition to the growth in transition economies, private business schools continue to feel the impact of the global mobility of students. The number of foreign students enrolled in US universities has grown to over a million, which is more than a 40% increase in the past decade (Kapadia, 2016). In the UK the number of international students is approximately 400,000 or about 19% of all university students. Other places such as Singapore are becoming popular international destinations for students who are interested in not just an educational experience but also a global cultural experience. This increasing international orientation has had an impact on the admissions and marketing efforts of business schools, which must now be operated increasingly at a global scale. Competition for top students continues to be a key challenge and the efforts to find and attract these students around the world results in additional costs and agency challenges as outlined in Chapter 2.

Operating budgets at private business schools have been increasing to address the additional complexity and volume in the admissions process as well as other student services such as careers. As noted in Chapters 2 and 3, the expectations of students concerning the quality of the education experience continue to increase. Operating budgets can also affect faculty hiring, time for research and staff support. Unlike public business schools, which are typically larger, private players have limited size and scale and may be constrained by resource limitations. Yet many private schools strive to provide the same offerings as the schools in other strategic groups. To strive to keep up with the competition, many private schools will offer an MBA, EMBA and other master's degree programmes even if the enrolment numbers are not significant. Table 5.3 shows a stylised model for a private business school. Here we note that no state funding is provided and the bulk of revenue comes from undergraduate programmes. Enrolment in the MBA and other master's programmes may depend on location as some private business schools in urban locations can be successful with part-time master's degree programmes. Unlike the elite schools, the draw for executive education is generally lower and likely more targeted at custom programmes for corporate partners.

The challenge for a private business school is often finding the right positioning in the changing higher education marketplace. This strategic group must carefully consider its options and work to align a school to meet that strategic intent. Without a clear market position, small private schools that lack healthy endowment funds must rely solely on tuition revenue, which poses significant risk in the event of falling enrolments. Several strategic options seem to emerge for private business schools depending on location, brand, and core competence.

Table 5.3. Example Revenue Sources for Private Institution Business School.

Program	Students	Annual Tuition	State Funding	Total Revenue
Undergraduates	2000	$35,000	$0	$70,000,000
Master's	400	$40,000	$0	$16,000,000
MBA	300	$45,000	$0	$13,500,000
EMBA	60	$70,000	$0	$4,200,000
PhD	40	$10,000	$0	$400,000
Exec Ed	2000	$3,000	$0	$6,000,000
				$110,100,000

For those private schools that operate in a thriving regional area, positioning as a strong undergraduate teaching school can be a positive strategic choice. In this case, a business school can offer smaller class sizes, increased attention to students by faculty and provide a positive learning experience for students. To be successful with this model, a school can place less emphasis on academic research, reduce graduate programme offerings and potentially create unique undergraduate experiences such as cross-disciplinary programmes within the university.

One such example is Butler University in Indiana in the US. With a 12-to-1 student-to-faculty ratio, the school accepts only 250 business school undergraduates each year. The business school is practice-oriented and leverages the nearby Indianapolis city business partner-ships to provide students with a positive and practical educational experience.

Striving for a specific niche focus is another strategic option for the private business school that may have a strong competency in a specific discipline or industry. Of course, consideration of the size and demand in the niche field is of critical important to avoid over-specialisation. Babson College in Massachusetts is an example of a private school with a niche focus on entrepreneurial skills and mindsets. With historic roots as a business education institute, it transformed in 2000 to focus on entrepreneurial education with an aim to be a "small school that does big things". While it admits less than 600 students to the undergraduate programme each year, it is one of the most competitive and successful small private business schools in the US.

With the advent of new teaching technologies and online learning, some private schools are aggressively moving into online programmes to achieve growth. This can provide additional options for revenue while avoiding physical facility costs. This can be especially important for private schools in urban settings as the physical space not only con-strains growth but also poses high costs. Pace University in New York City is a private school that offers online bachelor's business degrees. The business school has approximately 3,000 undergraduates and is constrained by space and rising costs in Manhattan. To maintain the strong faculty-to-student ratio and associated levels of interaction, each class has a maximum of 20 students with sessions scheduled in the eve-nings to allow students to work during the day. The online programmes allow Pace University to reach new groups of students and continue its growth.

Some private schools are also facing challenges with growth at the bachelor's level and are now extending the breadth of services to include associate degree programmes (Smith, 2016). Private schools with a strong community orientation may look for ways to entrench their offerings in the community served. For example, the University of St Thomas in Minnesota is launching a two-year associate degree programme for lower-income students who may not be ready or able to start with a traditional four-year bachelor's degree programme. While polytechnic schools or community colleges traditionally offer these programmes, some private schools are finding value in creatively filling the space before the traditional undergraduate experience while also helping to address the needs of the community that they serve.

Elite Business Schools

The elite business schools are a separate strategic group that face a different set of challenges and strategic options. This group is made up of those business schools that are consistently in the top 50 rankings and generally have a high level of demand and large endowment funds. Within the elite schools there is also a "super-elite" group in the US called the Magnificent Seven (M7). The leaders of these business schools meet regularly to compare ideas and information on the industry. The M7 members include Harvard, Stanford, U Penn Wharton, Northwestern Kellogg, Chicago Booth, Columbia and MIT Sloan. In Europe, schools such as INSEAD, LBS, IMD, IESE, IE and HEC also form a cadre of well-ranked, elite schools. In Asia, HKUST, CEIBS, NUS, SMU and ISB form a collaborative network seeking to better understand the dynamics of the industry in the region.

Global elite business schools compete aggressively for both MBA candidates and MBA rankings. Recruiting at this level typically involves an aggressive use of scholarships. The top 25 business schools in the US spend more than $200 million in scholarships for MBA students (Baron & Allen, 2014). As shown in Chapter 3, the competition for top students involves aggressive marketing, strong admissions processes and an active alumni network.

Rankings have created a fundamental shift in the orientation of business schools since they are largely focused on MBA programmes and the results have a significant impact on the quality of the applications, the enrolment levels in executive education and even undergraduate application quality. The rankings game can be a virtuous cycle of maintaining happy alumni (who are surveyed as a part of the ranking process), the right balance of faculty and high placement results. For the elite schools, maintaining and improving their ranking scores is a critical activity that involves significant resources each year. Without top rankings, the elite schools will not be able to attract top students.

To aid their competition for recruiting the best students and creating a positive student experience, elite schools have access to strong endowment funds. These funds are generally professionally managed to maximise annual returns. The strong schools may use a portion of the earnings each year to help pay for scholarships or other variable costs. This access to capital is not easy to obtain and can quickly become a competitive advantage. The endowment at Harvard Business School, for example, is currently valued at around $3.3 billion while other elite US schools follow with endowments in the hundreds of millions to over a billion dollars (Stanford and Wharton).

In Europe, giving from alumni is not so common and is not facilitated by tax incentives as it is in the US. Thus, European elite schools typically have smaller endowments and therefore less flexibility and financial strength in the event of a downturn. As such, prominent schools such as INSEAD and London Business School have endowment funds of $195 million and $58 million respectively (Bonsoms, 2016). Growing endowment funds is a major activity in elite business schools as marketing and brand-promotion activities take centre stage in reinforcing their strategic positioning.

Managing the brand is of critical importance to elite schools. First, schools must work to protect their brands by preventing others infringing on school logos, trademarks or names. Elite brands are sought after around the world and the corner bookstores on elite school campuses can often be filled with tourists looking for a shirt or souvenir carrying the name of the business school. While these are harmless and even helpful promotions of the brand, there is often a more serious side to abusing the brands of elite schools

Consider one school in China that offers prospective students a chance to study at "London Business School" for a portion of the programme that they are offering, without the knowledge or consent of the genuine LBS. The students study in China for most of the programme and then make a trip to London for a week or two. Organisers may rent space at a hotel or small education centre to hold "LBS Classes" given by a local person (not from LBS) and may give the students a short tour of the campus as well as a free T-shirt. Some of these questionable programmes may even create "certificates" for the completion of the study.

This form of brand abuse is not uncommon and often hard to prevent. However, elite brands are powerful and the schools are constantly working to protect their brands and restrict the use of the school name and logo. This can be increasingly complex as many of these schools work to set up global partnerships to extend their brand to other regions, as discussed in Chapter 6.

The stylised revenue model for an elite school is shown in Table 5.4. Elite schools can generally command high tuition fees and will have large programme numbers. The top elite schools regularly accept between 500 to 800 MBA students each year, which creates a significant portion of the revenue (at healthy margins) enjoyed by a school. While revenue is significantly higher for these schools than it is for other strategic groups, the expectations of the student experience is also much higher. Therefore, the administrative costs can be significant, not only to address student processes but also support the ongoing global marketing, alumni relationships, brand affiliations and rankings processes.

As a strategic group, elite business schools have been very successful in establishing a strong reputation for, and track record of, success. Over the last decade, elite schools have been hypercompetitive in achieving their relative positions in the *Financial Times* rankings each year in hopes of securing a long-term reputation for success. Yet changing demographics coupled with waning interest in the traditional two-year full-time MBA programmes may create some future challenges. In addition, elite business schools must also be prudent in addressing risk management to protect their long-term interests and success.

Table 5.4. Revenue Sources for Elite Institution.

Program	Students	Annual Tuition	State Funding	Total Revenue
Undergraduates	3000	$35,000	$0	$105,000,000
Master's	400	$60,000	$0	$24,000,000
MBA	1600	$80,000	$0	$128,000,000
EMBA	150	$90,000	$0	$13,500,000
PhD	80	$10,000	$0	$800,000
Exec Ed	5000	$4,000	$0	$20,000,000
				$291,300,000

One of the challenges facing the elite schools is how to improve their global reach. Some have set up small campuses in Asia, for example, to attract regional applicants (Chicago Booth in Singapore and subsequently in Hong Kong). While others have made strong commitments to creating multiple campuses (INSEAD and IMD). However, many of these schools continue to maintain a single main campus and hesitate to create satellite campus experiences for fear of diluting their brand image. Others have developed partnerships or dual programmes (Kellogg and HKUST). Yet other have created non-academic partnerships (MIT Sloan and Bank Negara Malaysia to create the Asia Business School in Kuala Lumpur). Managing alliance relationships can create new revenue sources and can extend the impact of the brand but also become a new challenge for elite schools as covered in Chapter 7.

Summary and Conclusions

During the decades prior to the rapid growth of business schools, most institutions found that it was relatively easy to expand their portfolios of offerings to include various forms of MBA programmes, executive education and other graduate programmes. Now that declining MBA enrolments and more competition for undergraduate students may limit new growth, business schools will need to re-evaluate their strategies.

As this chapter has illustrated, the strategic groups are relatively well defined in broad terms and provide a benchmark for decision-making options on strategic direction. We again note that while these strategic groups are used for classification purposes, these are over-generalisations of the many types and situations of business schools.

Using a broad-brush review, the strategic options for many publicly funded business schools may leverage the strength of these schools to provide education at scale, particularly at the undergraduate level. Private business schools have strategic options dictated by their locations and potential niche specialty areas while the elite schools must work to protect and expand their brands around the world.

Regardless of the strategic direction, each school will need to make portfolio choices related to management education such as executive education, graduate programmes, MBA and EMBA programmes, online programmes and potential alliances. Taking a resources-based view of each business school may yield unique options for competitive advantage that should be considered. It seems clear that as global and fast-paced competition increases, the current trend of standardised offerings and dominant paradigms across most business schools is not sustainable in the long-term. These hypercompetitive environments demand creativity in re-designing business models and re-orienting the value chains and practices of many schools.

References

Baade, R. A., & Sundberg, J. O. (1996). What determines alumni generosity? *Economics of Education Review, 15*(1), 75–81.

Baron, E., & Allen, N. (2014). The MBA scholarship wars. *Fortune.*

Bonsoms, D. (2016, April 4). *America's wealthiest business schools.* Retrieved September 2, 2017 from https://poetsandquants.com

Brustein, W. I. (2007). The global campus: Challenges and opportunities for higher education in North America. *Journal of Studies in International Education, 11*(3–4), 382–391.

Butrymowicz, S. (2012). In China, private colleges, universities multiply to meet higher-education demand. *The Hechinger Report.*

Campos, P. (2015). The real reason college tuition costs so much. *New York Times.* April 4.

Cappelli, P. (2015). *Will college pay off? A guide to the most important financial decision you'll ever make.* Canada: Public Affairs.

Denson, N., & Chang, M. J. (2009). Racial diversity matters: The impact of diversity-related student engagement and institutional context. *American Educational Research Journal, 46*(2), 322–353.

ICEF Monitor. (2015). *African summit calls for major expansion of higher education.* Retrieved from http://monitor.icef.com/

Kapadia, K. (2016, July 19). *How international students are keeping US colleges afloat and powering the tech industry.* Retrieved September 2, 2017 from www.TechCrunch.com

Kerr, C. (2001). *The uses of the university.* Cambridge, MA: Harvard University Press.

Khurana, R. (2007). *From higher aims to hired hands: The social transformation of American business schools and the unfulfilled promise of management as a profession.* Princeton, NJ: Princeton University Press.

Kraft, E., & Vodopoviec, M. (2003). The new kids on the block: The entry of private business schools in transition economies. *Education Economics, 11*(3), 239–257.

Levy, D. C. (2013). The decline of private higher education. *Higher Education Policy, 26*(1), 25–42.

Mintzberg, H. (2004). *Managers, not MBAs: A hard look at the soft practice of managing and management development.* San Francisco: Berrett-Koehler Publishers.

Muff, K. (2012). Are business schools doing their job? *Journal of Management Development, 31*(7), 648–662.

National Science Foundation. (2016). https://www.nsf.gov/nsb/sei/edTool/index. html. Accessed on 11 December 2016.

Newman, J. H. (1852). *The idea of a university*. London: Longmans Green.

Okunade, A. A., & Berl, R. L. (1997). Determinants of charitable giving of business school alumni. *Research in Higher Education, 38*(2), 201−214.

Pfeffer, J., & Fong, C. T. (2002). The end of business schools? Less success than meets the eye. *Academy of Management Learning & Education, 1*(1), 78−95.

Pfeffer, J., & Fong, C. T. (2004). The business school 'business': Some lessons from the US experience. *Journal of Management Studies, 41*(8), 1501−1520.

[The] Robbins Report. (1963). *Higher education: report of the committee appointed by the Prime Minister under the chairmanship of Lord Robbins, 1961-63* (No. 2). London: Her Majesty's Stationery Office.

Smith, A. (2016). Private universities branch into 2-year programs. *Inside Higher Ed*, 9 December 2016.

Thomas, H., Lorange, P., & Sheth, J. (2013). *The business school in the twenty-first century: Emergent challenges and new business models*. Cambridge, UK: Cambridge University Press.

Will, M. (2015). Giving to colleges rises nearly 11%. *The Chronicle of Philanthropy, 25*(5).

Wunnava, P. V., & Okunade, A. A. (2013). Do business executives give more to their alma mater? Longitudinal evidence from a large university. *American Journal of Economics and Sociology, 72*(3), 761−778.

Chapter 6

Innovation: Challenging the Business School in the VUCA World

Introduction

While the Ford and Carnegie reports sought to professionalise and bring a scientific eye to the teaching of management, they also generated two side-effects. The first was the removal of the "art and craft" of management from the curriculum. The second was the codification of a management curriculum that has become substantially fixed and where subjects are mostly taught as stand-alone courses (largely quantitative) that do not really reflect the actual practice of management.

We can all rattle off the core 10 or so courses that are to be found in most MBAs: macro and microeconomics, statistics, accounting, finance, operations, marketing, strategy, OB and HR. This codification was not handed down on tablets of stone and, equally, does not derive from the needs of practising managers. It comes from the departmentalisation of faculty members at business schools and the journals in which they publish. In practice, there is a dichotomy at work in almost all business schools between the "demand side" needs of the students – who seek to be well taught and hopefully to learn as much as possible about business (and get a good job) and the "supply side" orientation of faculty, whose careers are based on their academic output in highly regarded journals rather than the relevance, clarity and eloquence of their teaching.

Unfortunately, this codification is out of date in terms of what the future of work holds for students studying business courses at whatever level or depth. This chapter turns a fresh eye on the skills and abilities managers and leaders will require in order to be able to cope with new challenges. It also looks at the rethinking required around education generally and management development specifically. Too much of that thinking and what is taught within educational establishments, including business schools, looks backward as much as it looks forward (Laliani & Peters, 2015).

Looking at the practice of management and of management education will hopefully address some of the challenges that Henry Mintzberg

(2004), among others, has thrown down over past decades. It is time to recognise that existing approaches and models (including the dominant MBA paradigm) must change and adapt to fast-paced environmental conditions. A range of innovative models must be tried and implemented.

In the early 20th century, Henri Fayol, the classical management thinker, suggested that the work of managers was to "plan, organise, direct and control". Such notions now seem antiquated, and would be amusing were it not for the fact that there is a human tendency to seek simple answers. In a complex world, simplicity is seductive and simplification tools (which abound in the world of education) become dangerous when applied to strategic issues and problems because they apply a simple structure to an unstructured situation. What, then, are the implications for managers and management development?

"Complicate yourselves" is the battle cry offered by Weick (1979, p. 261), suggesting that managers need to be able to see and understand organisational events and behaviours from several perspectives rather than a single one. We are not futurologists but it seems to us that some key societal trends have become apparent that are critical for organisations and their managers. To give some insight, here is a synthesis of five such trends. While each is significant in itself, they are also interrelated, creating what has been called a "VUCA" world — one characterised by volatility, uncertainty, complexity and ambiguity.

Societal Trends, the VUCA World and Implications for Management Education

Disruptive Technology

The speed of innovation has accelerated to the point where entire industries are being reinvented in months and years rather than over decades. Various estimates exist about the extent to which the economy will change in the coming 10 to 20 years — and they are, of course, only estimates. That said, there are millions of hits on Google about this theme. Most come in at an estimate of 50% of present jobs disappearing by 2035 and, relatedly, a similar percentage of jobs of the future will be created that do not exist today.

Scaled-up from the employee perspective to the employer perspective, disruption — whether because of the disaggregation of value chains, the "gig" economy, big data and data analytics or simply innovation – is also upon us. Grossman (2016) posits that B2C industries, such as business schools, will be hardest and most imminently hit while industry will follow soon after.

Globalisation

The centre of gravity of the world economy has been shifting. Thanks to liberalisation and industrialisation, growth in emerging markets has transformed the world economy. We expect this trend to amplify. McKinsey authors (Dobbs, Ramaswamy, Stephenson, & Viguerie, 2014) suggest that "by 2025, emerging markets will have been the world's prime growth engine for more than 15 years, China will be home to more large companies than either the United States or Europe, and more than 45 per cent of the companies on *Fortune* magazine's list of the 500 largest corporations in the world, versus just 5 per cent in the year 2000."

Within emerging markets, populations are shifting from a rural, often agricultural, lifestyle to an urban society confronted by the challenges of growth. The global urban population is growing by 65 million people a year at present and with that growth comes income, the development of a consumer society and a revolution of rising aspirations, with old loyalties – to firms or to brands – often swept aside. This creates the need for a high degree of cultural as well as product-market adaptation for organisations and an increasing demand for producing multiculturally skilled, globally intelligent and adaptive managers. It also presents the challenge of a future world in which successful urban workers will be better educated by urban-based business schools while rural locations may well face unemployment, weaker educational standards, and poverty. The recent rise of populism seen in many countries (Brexit, Trumpism and so on) is directly linked to this trend.

Demographic Dynamics

Demographic shifts have long preoccupied policy makers. In the West, rising health-care costs and a lack of growth in the tax base due to an ageing population with increasing longevity have challenged the economics of welfare as well as the role of the state. In emerging markets, typically with younger populations, higher birth rates have fuelled concerns about appropriate levels of education growth and job creation. Most organisations, however, will have a mix of ages in the workplace.

This co-existence of different generations under one roof creates interesting challenges.

As Culpin, Millar, and Peters (2015) note, either because of legislative changes or, more prosaically, because savings rates are insufficient and pension plans inadequate for 25 years in retirement, individuals either need or choose to work more years than they previously expected to. From a workplace perspective, organisations thus face the challenge of both care for and utilisation of an ageing workforce. In addition, partly as a consequence of longer lives but also because of changing working conditions including the move away from life-long employment and toward more varied career patterns, there is significantly more movement in the workforce than previously.

Moving to the other end of the age spectrum, the younger workforce has incorporated this expectation of a portfolio career whilst simultaneously being skilled users of new technologies. In their curricula designs, organisations and business schools will need to adapt to multiple generations, each with a different set of expectations, needs, values, aspirations, skills and attitudes. Less predictable retirement ages, global working, a renewed focus on work and non-work balance as well as organisational well-being will all need to be managed within varying frames of reference. Leading and motivating people in such a context will inevitably become more challenging and require new managerial skills.

The Knowledge Economy

The people challenge becomes further magnified with the increasing dominance of the knowledge economy, in which the key assets of a business are not on the balance sheets and go home every night. Knowledge workers frequently combine expert knowledge with a high need for autonomy and a low regard for authority. Although innovation and collaboration are crucial, aligning organisational needs with the professional interests of knowledge workers is no easy task; indeed, "herding cats" is the somewhat disparaging expression the authors have encountered frequently.

While some work has been done on how to provide leadership for professional service firms, the arts and for R&D (Fragueiro & Thomas, 2011; Thomas, Lorange, & Sheth, 2013), it is generally acknowledged that managing for creative output is much harder than managing a smokestack business and needs to be better reflected in business school content. Further, it is genuinely impossible to know *a priori* if a creative knowledge worker will generate a subsequent great idea. One can consider an individual's track record and hope for the best but, as they say in the investment industry, "past performance is no indicator of future performance".

New Social Contract

Over the last decade, a weak signal of future change appears to have grown and moved centre-stage in many boardrooms. Since the appearance of the Stern Review of the Economics of Climate Change (Stern, 2007) in the UK, there has been an increasing preoccupation with issues of sustainability. Gitsham and Lenssen (2009) suggest that at a macro level, an increase in extreme weather and the associated problems of agricultural failure, water scarcity, disease and mass migration will bring forth crises on a scale we have never before witnessed. The Stern report, for example, extrapolated that climate change could swallow up to 20% of the world's GDP. At a micro level, the shift to a low-carbon economy to offset climate change is something that business leaders consider will be a key factor in coming years. Wider concerns relating to the sustainability of the natural environment − finite and increasingly scarce resources, energy, water, food, metals and minerals − also figure prominently.

The need to consider sustainable business models and create shared value (Porter & Kramer, 2011) means that organisations must consider not only their own product or service portfolio but also the broader effect of their activities on consumers and on society. A key element of this mix is not only the sustainability of the approach but also of the responsibility and ethical approach taken – both significant challenges for business school curriculum design. In practice, this requires organisations to build and maintain trust within their value chain and with their stakeholder groups, all within a climate of ever-increasing scrutiny and transparency. Leaders will need to understand this changing business context and how their stakeholders − regulators, customers, suppliers, investors and NGOs − factor social and environmental trends into their strategic decision making, creating thought-provoking issues for the design of leadership development programmes (Carlile et al., 2016).

Such significant trends as digital disruption, big data and concomitant analytical approaches, globalisation, sustainability, knowledge work and demographic shifts mean that having a narrow framework is simply insufficient.

The need for multiple lenses and perspectives is recognised by CEOs. In a study as early as 2008, carried out with 200 CEO respondents from around the world by Gitsham and Lenssen, 76% thought it important for senior leaders in their own organisations to have the mindset, skills and abilities to lead in a holistic manner yet only 8% believed that these skills were present at the moment. There is, therefore, a clear leadership deficit.

Needed Skills and Capabilities in the VUCA World

Managers in the future will require capabilities in four broad clusters:

Contextual Mastery

All management is deeply contextual, meaning all organisations face a unique configuration of external (for example, competitive setting and life cycle) and internal environments (for example, culture and systems). In effect, a context is a type of situation wherein particular structures, relationships, processes and competitive settings can be found (Mintzberg & Quinn, 1996).

> The practice of management, as evidenced in a lot of big corporations and banks, is utterly dreadful. I don't think business schools really get it, or care to get it. You can't create a manager in a classroom. Any effort or claim that they're creating managers by taking people who have never managed is fallacious....
>
> Management is a practice where art, craft and science meet. Craft is critically important because it's experience-based; art is fundamental to doing new things because it's creativity and insight-based; science is useful in the form of analysis, but we have very little scientific evidence of what works in management.
>
> (Mintzberg & Quinn, The Strategy Process: Concepts, Contexts, Cases, 1996).

It should be self-evident that what works in the cement industry may not work in the advertising industry or that the leadership style that works in a chemical plant may not work in a hospital although, paradoxically, most management ideas are presented as generic and universally applicable. Understanding the context and culture, and being sensitive to them, gives leaders credibility. However, understanding is not sufficient in itself: leaders must also challenge the meaning of context, and the paradigms and world views that characterise it, and explore how they might be changed.

Behavioural Complexity

Responding to complex demands in an uncertain and volatile environment requires managers to perform a wide array of leadership functions. They must build trusted relationships with a diverse range of people at different levels and mobilise, motivate, engage, and collaborate with and influence them. Being effective across a range of situations and time horizons requires of managers not only to have the ability to perceive the needs and goals of a constituency but also the ability to adjust based on the needs of group accordingly. (Brown & Eisenhardt, 1998; Kenny & Zaccaro, 1983, p. 678).

Behavioural complexity reflects the idea that managers who have a broad "bandwidth", or who perform multiple leadership functions, discern what is appropriate, and when, and can tailor their style, message, language and behaviour to the demands of the task, situation and role. And they will be more effective than managers who are relatively inelastic. A key premise is that the more complex a manager's behavioural repertoire, the more likely it is that the manager can respond effectively to the challenges at hand.

Judgement

Making the right choices in the face of conflicting processes, contending opposites and incomplete information requires the exercise of judgement. Paradoxes are a central feature of modern managerial life. Managers must deliver in the short term and in the long term. They must give autonomy but also ensure alignment. They must lead change but also provide stability and continuity. All these require conflicting actions. Numerous strategy and organisation researchers have pointed to the significant paradoxes that managers must work with. Paradoxes are not problems that must be solved but rather opposing positions that must be held meaningfully at the same time. For example, Mintzberg and Quinn (1996) emphasise the need to reconcile change and continuity. The manager must be a "pattern recogniser", with the ability to sense when to exploit established strategies and when to encourage new strains to displace the old. Jonas, Fry, and Srivastva (1990, p. 40) found that effective executives must "simultaneously embody the *status quo* and question it".

Self-efficacy

Leaders need high self-efficacy, which can be defined as an individual's belief in his or her capability to organise and execute the action required to attain desired performance levels. Psychologists suggest that it is an important variable that affects leader performance. Self-efficacy affects the thoughts, feelings and actions of individuals in several significant ways. According to Bandura's seminal work (1997), people with high self-efficacy approach difficult tasks as challenges to be mastered rather than as threats to be avoided. They set themselves challenging goals and remain committed to them in the face of adversity. They persist and heighten or sustain their efforts in the face of failure. They recover their sense of efficacy after setbacks, which they attribute to a lack of adequate effort or a lack of skills, which can be developed. Such a worldview supports personal accomplishments and reduces stress.

By contrast, people with low self-efficacy have low aspirations and are reluctant to take on difficult tasks. They demonstrate weak commitment to goals and are likely to abandon them if achievement proves difficult. They attribute unsatisfactory performance to deficiencies in their own aptitude. As a result, it does not require much failure for them to lose faith in their capabilities and they may suffer from stress and depression.

> *"The only thing that interferes with my learning is my education"* (Albert Einstein)

So how does development really happen and what does learning that goes beyond education look like?

Learning Beyond Education: Leadership Development in the VUCA World

At a basic level the purpose of learning and development is to cultivate cognitive and emotional maturity that allows individuals to be as aware and as thoughtful as possible about the consequences of their actions. According to Cook-Greuter (2004) there are two types of development: horizontal and vertical. Horizontal development, which refers to the acquisition of new skills and knowledge, is something "normal" life contributes to. Education combines with a maturation of abilities leading to a broader, albeit bounded, base. Most traditional development is horizontal. Vertical development, which is more potent, refers to a change in world-view and a transition to a higher level of maturity and sophistication. The former is largely triggered by external forces and comes to the individual, whereas the latter is sought by the individual and is largely driven internally through reflection.

Development interventions, when well designed, provide a combination of horizontal and vertical development and are characterised by novelty, reinforcement and repetition, and reflection and sense-making.

> *"Organizations must learn how to plan, and plan how to learn"* (Wooldridge & Floyd, 1990)

Seven Dilemmas for Management Education

In this new landscape, how can organisations best develop their most potent assets – their people? We believe that in the future, management education will need to address seven key dichotomies: Individual and Organisation; Cognitive and Behavioural; Action and Reflection; Theory and Practice; Teaching and Facilitation; Intellectual and Emotional Experiences; Formal and Informal Learning. While these are often presented as options or choices, in our experience each supports and underpins the other and it is therefore useful to consider how to integrate the elements of each dichotomy effectively.

Individual and Organisation

While much management education focuses on individuals, we believe this is necessary but not sufficient. We subscribe to the view that individual change is inseparable from organisational change. All learning is by definition subversive; it encourages people to challenge the *status quo*. Helping the individual to change, without paying any attention to the potentially unchanged environment into which the individual will return, is a waste of development effort. Equally, an organisational change process that does not explicitly consider the implications for the development needs of employees is unlikely to be sustainable over time. In any case, management development is a potent vehicle for organisational change and management development is most effective when it is accompanied by a process of organisational development. This twin focus on individual *and* organisation creates a symbiosis. It enables change that is directly linked to organisational needs, helps embed individual learning and creates workplace impact.

Cognitive and Behavioural

Knowing how to calculate the cost of capital, analyse market trends or design new product development process are rarely the biggest challenges that managers face. Of course these cognitive (or "knowing") skills are important (particularly for junior managers in semi-technical roles) and sense-making frameworks have an important role to play in shaping how individuals identify and process issues. But getting things done requires working with people. New products, budgets or strategies do not succeed or fail – people succeed or fail. As a result, behavioural (or "doing") skills are critical. While this divide is often framed as "hard" skills versus "soft" skills, a senior executive has rightly observed that "the soft stuff is harder than the hard stuff."

Action and Reflection

As Peter Drucker (1974) pointed out "the best plan is only good intentions, until it degenerates into work" (p.128). In other words, thinking must be translated into action. Organisations are generally designed for action and getting things done. But all too often this is characterised by an institutional bias against reflection, resulting in frequent "firefighting". At the other extreme, an excess of reflection with little action, creates the "paralysis by analysis" trap (Livingston, 1971). In managers and their development both conditions of thinking and acting must be present. Thinking must be translated into action and action must inform thinking. Reflection helps us to gain new insights, converting implicit knowledge into actionable knowledge. In turn, patterns of action help create "muscle memory" so that new ways of thinking and behaving become seemingly effortless.

Theory and Practice

Managers often give a bad press to theory, dismissing it as irrelevant and impractical. Ironically, most managers do not realise that they are constant users of theory. Right or wrong, managerial actions are based on beliefs about which actions will lead to what consequences and why – in other words, an implicit theory. Good theory helps us to predict as well as to understand (Christiansen & Raynor, 2003). Managers therefore need good theory; and the divide between theory and practice is potentially spurious. Indeed, it has even been suggested that "there is nothing so practical as a good theory" (Lewin, 1951). Recognising that theory can often be generic, managers should be helped to learn to explore, adapt and deploy it in their own unique context.

Teaching and Facilitation

Teaching and facilitation are complex professions; together they help make the learning experience "sticky" and impactful. Many of us have had the privilege of great teachers; we recall them vividly years later. Good teachers provide authoritative expertise and distinctive points of view; they engage, challenge, stimulate, inspire and make learning fun. Teachers help make managers discerning consumers of management ideas.

Good facilitators are skilled in group dynamics, and can help groups of managers by organising the learning journey and providing individual support and feedback. Facilitators work with groups to co-create the learning and orchestrate discovery, a role that should not be underestimated given the wealth of experience that is frequently found in the learner side of the room. Effective management education therefore needs both the "sage on the stage" as well as the "guide on the side".

Intellectual and Emotional Experiences

Well-crafted management education enables participants to stretch outside their comfort zones and confront new challenges in a safe and supportive environment as well as prepare for the unexpected and learn to manage the anxieties, stresses and pressures of an uncertain and ambiguous world. While tidy classroom abstractions and intellectual debate have their value, visceral development experiences that represent an emotional stretch are a crucial driver of development.

Formal and Informal Learning

Profound and enduring development happens from experience. The workplace provides myriad opportunities for development. The informal learning that happens on the job is potent and immediately relevant to an individual's context. However, it can also be risky, inconsistent, high cost, and inaccurate and unchallenged.

Formal learning through deliberately designed interventions, on the other hand, can mitigate some of the inefficiencies of informal learning. Formal learning is scalable and explicit and lends itself to customisation. It provides opportunities for informal benchmarking, reflection, learning from peers and converting tacit knowledge to explicit knowledge ("now I know what I know").

However, formal learning withers away when detached from the "day job". Ideally, therefore, we need well-thought-through strategies to integrate informal and formal learning. This requires an acknowledgement that real learning is not a "one-week fix" and a new perspective in which development begins on the job, well before a formal intervention starts, and continues back on the job well after the intervention has ended. Crafting "managed development experiences" is the challenge. If we accept that some of these premises and dilemmas are worth exploring further, then we must ask ourselves three basic questions about business schools and what they teach. First, who teaches? Second, what do they teach? And third, how is it taught.

Three Basic Questions

Who Teaches?

If management is a complex and multi-faceted challenge, then bringing practical experience into the classroom is surely an important element of management education. It is, however, not simply an exercise in bringing practitioners into the classroom as they often bring a single perspective with them along the lines of "this is how it works in my organisation". There is a larger role in management education for hybrid faculty − those who have either completed their postgraduate education and have gained practical managerial experience or who have reversed their experience by pursuing an academic bridge programme such as a DBA at a mid-career point. Whatever the manner, practice and abstraction can be suitably combined.

As noted in an earlier chapter, some specialisation between teaching and research can have considerable financial implications for a business school. This is not to propose a complete dichotomy where research and teaching are separate streams of activity but we would suggest that a continuum with different research and teaching loads would be appropriate for business education overall. It does mean that schools must develop a more sophisticated reward system and that pracademics would also need opportunities for advancement — but this cannot be beyond the wit of humanity or designers of business school incentive systems.

What Do They Teach?

Teaching business education through faculty departments organised according to disciplines, which themselves are related to external journals, is clearly more in the interest of faculty members than of students or participants. In the real world, management is a continuous process that crosses discipline lines and involves myriad roles and functions — bringing a new product to market, expanding internationally, implementing severe cost cutting, the list goes on. But teaching along process lines is a challenge for business schools since it involves presenting multidisciplinary perspectives involving many diverse faculty to team teach and work together on curriculum issues. At the level of degree programmes, this means that the curriculum takes on a thematic rather than a subject area perspective. Happily, a number of programmes are now being designed in this manner.

Certainly at the level of executive education, this guiding principle is evident in interventions that seek to drive change and innovation in the workplace. Additionally, as pressure increases from executive education clients to show genuine impact, demand for hybrid faculty members who can combine intellectual rigour with practical relevance increases exponentially.

How Do They Teach?

Earlier, this chapter pointed to technological progress and innovation. The logical outflow for business schools is to reflect on the substance of the art, craft and science of business education from an additional perspective — namely, how one can deliver each element in the most rational, efficient and cost-effective manner?

If we equate the science element of the equation to the transfer of a body of knowledge from a source to a recipient or from one generation to another much can be delivered through technological enabling. Call it online learning, the internet, a MOOC or reading a book on a device, much can be achieved in this manner. It surely is not a rational use of faculty resources to teach absolutely basic level anything to anyone in a business school environment. Flipping the classroom − in other words ensuring that access to knowledge is predominantly prepared outside of the classroom with the actual class session based on sense-making and discussion − must be the way to go.

This effectively means that class time is used as much as possible to focus on the art and craft of education. Mintzberg's caveats about the difficulty of learning real-world skills in an artificial environment such as a classroom obviously need to be kept in mind but there are still many opportunities to use classroom time for the development of the softer people skills that are critical to managerial careers. Simulations, live cases, working groups, guest speakers − a range of opportunities are available to the thoughtful educator.

Being creative with sourcing material is also something that needs to be considered from a different perspective. There is a tendency for business schools to be comfortable with assigning books, cases and other written work from various authors at a multitude of different, often competing, business schools. Yet when it comes to creating online learning material, there is a strange anchor of the past. For example, schools almost always only use their own faculty members as video lecturers in emulation of the "live" experience. Surely the logic of education in the 21st century is that we as educators are as much curators of the best material, no matter where it has been produced in the digital and/or analogue world. One would think that by integrating extensive material from other schools, from news organisations and from other online sources such as TED and YouTube in a way we rarely do at present is both logical and suitable for the future of business education.

Summary and Conclusions

While there may be many challenges and pressures on the business of management education, this chapter has sought to provide encouragement for business school professionals to look at our industry with fresh eyes. It has presented puzzle pieces, or probably a better analogy would be Lego bricks, from both the programmatic and business elements of an overall school structure. A puzzle indicates that there is a "right solution"; Lego, on the other hand, allows for a whole range of options. What gets built really depends on what is realistic for a particular school. Determining what makes sense requires a school to reflect deeply on a whole range of factors perhaps using a resource-based view of the firm (Wernerfelt, 1984) or a similar wide-ranging thought exercise.

Questions abound. Where is a school and what does the environment support? Is a school in a location that is attractive for postgraduate programmes and executive education or is it more suited to residential undergraduate programmes? What is the predominant language of the school and if it is not English or perhaps Spanish does the school seek to expand internationally? What are the demographics of the regional or national population? What price points are appropriate for programmes and are there any sources of financial support from the state or from other bodies? Is there specific content expertise generated through the research of the faculty? If the financial resources to support a research-intensive business school are not available, what positioning is realistic for a teaching-intensive school? Does a school seek to have permanent faculty at all? Does it seek to dispense with faculty altogether (no laughing, please) and deliver only through internet-based online learning? Is accreditation and a relatively high standing in the various business school rankings necessary to make the overall business plan work?

At the end of the day, there are many paths to success but the critical path is that there is alignment between the strategy and the ability to deliver on that strategy. As noted in earlier chapters, specific and very different skill sets, content and environmental factors are required in the undergraduate, postgraduate and executive education arenas. What a school offers to the market place is something that real-life students and executive education clients must be willing to participate in and pay for in sufficient numbers that ensure the financial viability and stability of a school.

Many of the 13,000 or so business schools in the world have found models that work while others, as we have described, have struggled and have closed, merged or restructured. It is the belief of the authors that due to globalisation, technology, demographics, the knowledge economy and the need for a sustainable planet, we will see more volatility in the coming years than we have in previous decades. The next chapter will look at some schools that have restructured and others that we believe are tackling the future in interesting ways.

References

Bandura, A. (1997). *Self-efficacy: The exercise of control.* New York: W H Freeman.

Brown, S. L., & Eisenhardt, K. M. (1998). *Competing on the edge.* Cambridge, MA: Harvard Business School Press.

Carlile, P. R., Davidson, S. H., Freeman, K. W., Thomas, H., & Venkatraman, N. (2016). *Reimagining business education: Insights and actions from the business education jam.* Bingley, UK: Emerald Group Publishing Limited.

Christiansen, M. C., & Raynor, M. E. (2003). Why hard-nosed executives should care about management theory. *Harvard Business Review, 81*(9), 66−74.

Cook-Greuter, S. R. (2004). Making the case for a developmental perspective. *Industrial and Commercial Training, 36*(7), 275−281.

Culpin, V., Millar, C., & Peters, K. (2015). Multi-generational frames of reference: Managerial challenges of four social generations in the organisation. *Journal of Managerial Psychology, 30*(1).

Dobbs, R., Ramaswamy, S., Stephenson, E., & Viguerie, P. (2014). Management intuition for the next 50 years. *McKinsey Quarterly, 3rd Quartley,* (3), 12−24.

Drucker, P. F. (1974). *Management: Tasks, responsibilities, practices.* London: William Heinemann.

Fragueiro, F., & Thomas, H. (2011). *Strategic Leadership in the business school: Keeping one step ahead.* Cambridge, UK: Cambridge University Press.

Gitsham, M., & Lenssen, G. (2009). Developing the global leader of tomorrow. *Ashridge Business School and European Academy of Business in Society Report.*

Grossman, R. (2016). The industries that are being disrupted the most by digital. *Harvard Business Review.*

Jonas, H., Fry, R., & Srivastava, S. (1990). The office of the CEO: Understanding the executive experience. *Academy of Management Executive, 4*(3), 36−48.

Kenny, D. A., & Zaccaro, S. J. (1983). An estimate of variance due to traits in leadership. *Journal of Applied Psychology, 68*(4), 678−685.

Laljani, N., & Peters, K. (2015). The future of management development: Some reflections. In P. Hind (Ed.), *Management development that works.* London: Libri Publishing.

Lewin, K. (1951). *Field theory in social science: Selected theoretical papers.* In D. Cartwright (Ed.). New York: Haper & Row.

Livingston, J. S. (1971). Myth of the well-educated manager. *Harvard Business Review, 49*(1), 79−89.

Mintzberg, H. (2004). *Managers, not MBAs: A hard look at the soft practice of managing and management development.* San Francisco, CA: Berrett-Koehler Publishers.

Mintzberg, H., & Quinn, J. B. (1996). *The strategy process: Concepts, contexts, cases* (3rd ed.). Englewood Cliffs, NJ: Prentice-Hall.

Porter, M. E., & Kramer, M. R. (2011). Creating shared value. *Harvard Business Review, 89*(1/2), 62−77.

Stern, N. H. (2007). *The economics of climate change: The Stern review.* Cambridge, UK: Cambridge University Press.

Thomas, H., Lorange, P., & Sheth, J. (2013). *The business school in the twenty-first century.* Cambridge, UK: Cambridge University Press.

Weick, K. E. (1979). *The social psychology of organizing.* Reading, UK: Addison-Wesley.

Wernerfelt, B. (1984). The resource-based view of the firm. *Strategic Management Journal, 5*(2), 171–180.

Wooldridge, B., & Floyd, W. (1990). The strategy process, middle management involvement, and organizational performance. *Strategic Management Journal, 11*(3), 231–241.

Chapter 7

New Entrants, Strategic Alliances and Business Schools Closures

Introduction

Business schools contained within large university systems have been relatively sheltered from major disruptions as they are generally protected by a large, more stable, university infrastructure. Stand-alone business schools, on the other hand, have been much more dynamic in recent years. This chapter examines changes that have taken place not within a particular element of the value chain of a business school but changes of structure and of control that have altered the circumstances of a school overall. Later parts of this chapter will look at the drivers for change in a systematic manner and will attempt to group changes of business school structures into a number of categories. Finally, it suggests that some types of changes are more likely to be successful than others.

Mergers, Acquisitions and Alliances

Rather than attempt to describe each merger in depth, the goal is to present a categorisation akin to a strategic group clustering of corporate strategies. There are a number of mergers that have taken place in the past few decades (Brown, 2014) and this chapter addresses some of the drivers that brought schools together and some of the issues they have faced subsequently or potentially may face in the future.

In examining the overall range of mergers and acquisitions, a number of drivers can be identified. One, obviously, is a need for financial resources on the part of one or both of the actors (Lindsay, 2015). The logic is that there are scale benefits in combining operations and that these economies of scale, and also perhaps economies of scope, across all or many of the elements in the value chain will generate more surplus revenue. In looking at the value chain, there is potential for synergy in everything from sales and marketing through to back office services, from housing through to placement and from teaching full classrooms rather than sub-optimal programme attendance numbers. In cases where both schools are geographically in the same location, there is the additional potential benefit of a rationalisation of the overall business school estate.

There are a number of organisations that have pushed the model of acquisition further than simply acquiring one partner. Laureate, and more recently Global University Systems (GUS), have been using sales and marketing and back office scale benefits to create entire eco-systems of acquired schools (GUS, 2016; Kalia, 2015). In both cases, a sales and marketing capacity in terms of sales staff and the sophistication of online and social media marketing have been able to generate an impact that is far superior to the historical capacity of the acquired schools. A second driver for consolidation is the upside potential of "strength in numbers" (Mitchell, 2015). A business school can increase its footprint through a merger by benefitting from the overall increase in programme and research capacity that arises from the addition of the second school's product and service range (Nguyen, 2015). Additionally, it is possible to extend geographic range by tying up with a school in a new and strategically important location.

The drivers and activities cited above assume that both merging business schools are in a position to decide their own destiny. For many, if not most real or potential mergers, that assumption of freedom is a fallacy because quite often the potential partners are the business schools of a university. This adds an additional layer of complexity to the potential of the alliance.

Context and Background

Previous chapters have looked at the changes brought to the higher-education system within the broader European landscape through the introduction of the Bologna Accord in the late 1990s and early 2000s. A brief detour into the pre-Bologna landscape helps understand subsequent developments.

In almost all of the Bologna signatory countries – the UK and Ireland being the main exceptions – the first degree that students could complete was the hybrid bachelor's/master's described earlier and called a *Diplom-Kaufmann* in Germany, a *Doctorandus* in the Netherlands, a *Licenciado* in Spain and so on. Specific bachelor's programmes were not a part of the educational system and nor were MBAs, EMBAs and direct-entry specialist master's programmes. There was, nevertheless, both student demand and university or business school ambition to be involved in these well-known and seemingly lucrative types of study. Thus through the 1970s and more generally in the 1980s, a whole range of universities, as well as freestanding new market entrants, launched MBAs and similar US-style degees (Pettigrew, Cornuel, & Hommel, 2014). Where a university was involved, this often led to a dual educational stream. The first stream was the state-funded, nationally recognised "proper" education, geerally in the country's national language, while the second was an internationally oriented, US-modelled, fee-charging parallel school, often taught in English, and which fell outside of the purview of national regimes and existed in a relatively free space of its own. In many cases, there were no specific national laws governing an MBA programme nor a national quality control regime that reviewed such programmes because they were not state funded and were thus outside state monitoring systems.

When Bologna was introduced and the progression from bachelor's to master's to doctoral level became the European as well as the North American and rest-of-the-world norm, having two parallel institutions within the same university did not make much sense. Universities decided that having one business school on campus was preferable to having two and invariably the more autonomous, innovative, entrepreneurial, freedom-loving US-modelled school was shotgun married into the publicly funded, painfully bureaucratic, ponderous, sterile no-fun school. If the reader detects any sort of value judgment in the previous sentences, perhaps based on a personal experience, that would be entirely inappropriate and purely coincidental.

For the above reasons, as well as the obvious perception that business schools tend to be part of universities, the role of the overall university is also key to the mergers and acquisitions landscape. So, besides the changes brought on specifically by the campus house-keeping described above, what has happened in the previous few decades and how does one make sense of it all?

Business School and Business School Mergers

a. *Switzerland: International Management Institute (IMI) and Institut pour l'Etude des Methodes de Direction de l'Entreprise (IMEDE) becomes Institute of Management Development (IMD), 1990*

The goal of the creation of IMD, one of the first business school mergers we are aware of, is amply described in the doctoral dissertation by Fernando Fragueiro and the subsequent book co-authored with Howard Thomas (2011). While all changes of structure and control seek to generate numerous benefits, in the case of IMD the most significant driver was a desire for scale.

b. *France: Ceram and ESC Lille become Skema, 2009*

In France, the wind of inevitable government reforms was felt by 2007. Both CERAM, a business school run by the General Assembly of the French Riviera Chamber of Commerce and Industry, and ESC Lille, an association under the French 1901 law, both saw the Bologna changes – increased competition and shrinking chamber of commerce budgets – as a threat to their survival. They knew that strategically they would have to find a way to survive minus the levels of historical funding (Guilhon, 2015). The merger thus can be classified as a desire both for economies of scale and scope.

c. *France: BEM Bordeaux and Euromed become Kedge, 2012*

In 2012 BEM Bordeaux and Euromed merged to create KEDGE (Kedge Business School, 2012; Smith, 2012). Economies of scale, a greater ability for international marketing and a desire for overall expansion drove the merger (Econostrum.info, 2013).

d. *France: Reims and Rouen become NEOMA, 2013*

NEOMA Business School was created in 2013 out of a merger of two well-respected French business schools: Rouen Business School and Reims Management School. Both schools were financed by their local chambers of commerce. As with other French schools financed by their local chambers, subsidies were decreasing and competition was increasing. The schools had already been co-operating in a joint venture that had created a Paris presence from 2009 (Bradshaw, 2013 August). Merging the schools was a natural continuation of the co-operation, which also sought growth to increase visibility internationally.

e. *Ashridge (UK) and Hult (US) 2015*

The drivers for the Ashridge-Hult merger were complex but complementary. For Ashridge, greater scale was required to afford the costs of maintaining both a historical property and historical pension liabilities. Additionally, in a globalised market for executive education, a global network of campuses was desirable (Hult News, 2015).

Hult was created initially through the acquisition of Arthur D Little Management Initiative in Boston in 2003 (as described later in this chapter). At this point, Hult's challenges were two-fold. In order to strengthen the school's positioning as a business school close to business, executive education was needed. Similarly, expanding the research portfolio to include research aimed at working professionals would be valuable.

f. *Netherlands: TIAS and NIMBAS, 2006*

A merger different than any of the others discussed above, TIAS Nimbas Business School in the Netherlands came about as a result of a 100% acquisition of shares of the Universiteit NIMBAS in Utrecht by Tias Business School, the business school associated with Tilburg University and Eindhoven University of Technology (TiasNimbas, 2009). The merger was a takeover because the founder of NIMBAS sought to retire and cash out of the educational venture.

g. *CEIBS (China) and Lorange (Switzerland) 2016*

CEIBS was established in 1994 under an agreement between the Ministry of Foreign Trade and Economic Co-operation (MOFTEC, now The Ministry of Commerce) and the European Commission through EFMD. The choice of Switzerland was important to CEIBS because it is situated in the centre of Europe and had a high attractiveness ranking. "The clear aim of this deal is for dominant Chinese practices - such as long-term time horizons, consensus management, etc - to be shared with European audiences, where there is already a genuine interest" (Wanot, 2015). The Lorange story is similar to that of NIMBAS, with the founder of the school withdrawing over time and passing the school on to other hands.

Business school and business school mergers obviously require sufficient autonomy on the part of the players to act in their own interests. In reviewing the list above, and perhaps because of a knowledge bias on behalf of the authors, there is a preponderance of schools based in France and other schools in Europe. This is largely because of a long-standing European tradition of having stand-alone business schools. In France, they were largely founded and funded by local chambers of commerce and supported by the state controlled *taxe d'apprentissage*, which encouraged life-long study. Alas, by the late 2000s, chambers of commerce, under increasing financial pressure, looked to their local business schools and could not always see the direct link between the school and the local community. French business schools had become national players, while chambers of commerce remained geographically rooted. Cost cutting by the chambers led to consolidation by the schools. In the above examples where two schools merged, there has been an after-life. In the case of one example we have not described in detail, an attempt was made in 2012 to merge four schools and six locations to form France Business School. The ambition was grander than the ability to deliver. We cannot say we are surprised.

Business Schools and Universities with Business School Mergers

h. *Henley (UK) and University of Reading (UK), 2008*
The merger of Henley Management College and Reading University in 2008 is a good example of how a merger between a stand-alone business school and a university-based business school presents challenges and benefits. Henley realised that competition was increasing in key markets such as the distance-learning MBA; that executive education demand would reduce due to the 2008 recession; and that there was little market space for small and medium-sized business schools (Independent Online, 2011). With very few portfolio overlaps, Reading provided the asset base of a bigger partner, was a leading research university and had strong contacts in Asia, Africa and India. What Reading lacked were the market-facing corporate relations that Henley had (Anderson, 2008).

i. *Thunderbird and Arizona State University (US) 2014*
In 2013, the US-based Thunderbird School of Global Management was in a difficult financial position, ending the fiscal year with a loss of $8.7 million, more than double that of the previous year. The offer of a merger with Arizona State University came as a much-needed lifeline, giving Thunderbird respite from the burden of its losses (Clark, 2014). While Thunderbird's strategic motivations for the merger were evident, ASU's intentions were far less clear, given that it already had the WP Carey School of Business. When asked about the benefits of the merger to both universities, ASU President Michael M Crow said "through the integration of Thunderbird with ASU, the Thunderbird historic global education vision will be sustained and extended, students at ASU and Thunderbird will have access to more courses and programs, ASU's executive education programs can be broadened and expanded, and financial efficiencies will be created" (Wiles & Ryman, 2014).

j. *Manchester consolidation between Manchester Business School (UK), Victoria University of Manchester (UK), and University of Manchester Institute of Science and Technology (UK) 2004 – the business school has since been renamed Alliance Manchester Business School*

The "new" Manchester Business School was formed in 2004 as a result of the merger of UMIST's Manchester School of Management, the Institute of Innovation Research (IoIR), the Victoria University's School of Accounting and Finance, and the "old" Manchester Business School. The merger was not instigated by the business schools but came about as the result of the creation of the University of Manchester, which sought to streamline higher education in the Manchester conurbation and to achieve notable scale. In 2015, Manchester Business School changed its name to Alliance Manchester Business School following a donation from the Alliance family (Hall, 2004).

k. *Melbourne Business School (Australia) and the University of Melbourne (Australia) attempted a consolidation in 2009, which instead turned into a "collaboration"*

The history of Melbourne Business School provides examples of a variety of types of structural change. In 2004, Melbourne Business School Limited merged with Mt Eliza Business School, which had been established in 1957 effectively as a provider of executive education. In Melbourne proper, discussions took place throughout the 2000s between Melbourne Business School and the University of Melbourne's business faculty to provide greater clarity for business education in the city of Melbourne (Buckridge, 2009). Merger discussions were cancelled in 2009 as no agreements could be reached (Gluyas & Trounson, 2009; Tomazin, 2009). By 2013, discussions were on again but with proposals for a structure whereby MBS merged with the faculty of business and economics in the University of Melbourne but retained control over significant elements of governance. In this agreement, MBS remains independent yet collaborates freely as a part of the University of Melbourne (Bradshaw, 2013).

l. *AGSM (Australia) 1999 and 2005*

The Australian School of Graduate Management was established with federal government resources as the New South Wales' second school of postgraduate management studies but as a national management school (similar to LBS and WBS in the UK) following the Jackson Report. In January 1999, the AGSM and the Graduate School of Business of the University of Sydney merged under the AGSM brand to form a joint venture between the two parties. In November 2005, the University of Sydney senate voted to opt out of this joint venture with AGSM. AGSM returned to the full ownership of UNSW. A year later, UNSW merged AGSM with the UNSW Faculty of Commerce and Economics, creating the Australian School of Business (for a brief period, the new faculty was called the Faculty of Business). Thus the AGSM as a business unit ceased operations although courses under the AGSM brand continued within the Faculty of Business (Potter, 2005).

m. *Finland: Aalto University (Finland) consolidating Helsinki University of Technology, University of Art and Design Helsinki and Helsinki School of Economics, 2010*

A merger created with the idea of bringing together science and technology, design and art, and business and economics under one brand, Aalto University is a combination of the Helsinki School of Economics, Helsinki University of Technology and the University of Art and Design Helsinki. The university began operations on 1 January 2010. The merger aimed to tackle the poor performance of Finland's universities relative to its top-ranking school-level tests (Tienari, Aula, & Aarrevaara, 2016). "The new university was designed to put innovation and impact on the knowledge economy at the heart of things," said Aalto's vice president, Hannu Seristo (Aalto University, 2016).

n. *US-based Cornell University consolidating School of Applied Economics and Management, the Johnson Graduate School of Management and the School of Hotel Administration, 2016*

Cornell announced in January 2016 that it would merge the Charles H Dyson School of Applied Economics and Management, the Samuel Curtis Johnson Graduate School of Management and the School of Hotel Administration "to establish an integrated College of Business with the transformative excellence, scope and scale to cement the University's position as a world-class center of teaching and research for business management and entrepreneurship" (Cornell, 2016). Cornell sees an opportunity to become the country's number-one business school and at the same time retain its schools' separate identities. The consolidation will allow them to recruit top faculty and students together instead of to discrete accredited institutes working against each other (Kelly, 2016).

In business school / university mergers there are two main drivers at play. In the first two cases, where Henley merged with Reading in the UK and where Thunderbird merged with Arizona State University in the US, Henley and Thunderbird opted for the support and scale available from a large university. In all mergers and acquisitions there is a larger party and a smaller party, a richer party and a poorer party. Whoever has the size and the money makes the rules. In both of these cases, the autonomy of a formerly free-standing business school has not only been compromised through the involvement of a business school at the university but that the university calls the shots for the newly merged entity.

It is not our role to say whether business school mergers are good or bad and how one might judge, some years later, whether the essence of a school has subsequently changed. Suffice it to say that the double cultural change from independence through to merger, with the weight of a university on top of it all, leads to a more significant cultural change than the merger of two business schools.

The second set of mergers in which a university takes the lead are consolidation plays either within a multi-activity, multi-business school environment or within a city or region. The Dutch and Finnish examples above were largely driven by the consequences of Bologna and a desire to create a simpler, single-school environment. The US, UK and Australian examples show consolidation at a level up from single university house-cleaning to city-wide or regional bundling. Having seen both the Manchester and Melbourne processes roll-out first-hand in an advisory role, it quickly became evident that consolidating on a grand scale is a difficult endeavour. Creating a new joined-up culture from myriad disparate elements with different world-views, prompted not by the business school but by a university, is no mean feat. The Manchester consolidation went through. In the Melbourne case, the business school dug its heels in and would not, ultimately, join the university.

Business Schools Purchasing a University

o. *Acquisition of SEK University by IE University 2004*
As a result of the introduction of Bologna and the concomitant move to a holistic higher education framework, a number of business schools found themselves in need of a licence to practise in their national jurisdictions. In Spain, regulators approved bylaw changes for SEK University in 2004 and authorised its partial sale to IE University (owner of the IE Business School) in 2006. SEK University officially changed its name to IE University in 2008. IE University, previously a purely postgraduate institution, had been expanding in terms of departments and international presence as well as increasingly introducing technology within its teaching methods. It acquired SEK University to open doors to SEK's global

undergraduate student body. It began operations as IE University in September 2009 (IE University, 2017).

p. *US-based Hult International Business School buying Huron University USA in London in 2007 after having bought the Arthur D Little Business School in Boston in 2003*

In 2003, when the not-for-profit Arthur D Little Business School in Boston in the US was threatened by the financial difficulties of its parent consultancy business, Bertil Hult, the founder of the language-training company EF, rescued the school and renamed it Hult International Business School in 2003 (Bradshaw, 2004). The school had NEASC (New England Association Schools and Colleges) permission to provide master's-level degree programmes. Subsequently, Hult International Business School went on to buy Huron University as a means of further expansion into undergraduate education.

The concept of a business school acquiring a university appears counter-intuitive at first. However, the driver of the acquisition is clear: universities have licences to practise in their particular jurisdictions. Licences to practise are also transferable. And licences to practise, especially in the US, come up more often than one might imagine.

Business Schools Purchased by Private Equity or Corporates

q. *US-based Apollo Education Group buys UK-based BPP, 2009 – and US-based Apollo Management Group buys Apollo Education Group, 2016*

In 2009, Apollo Education Group, the owner of the University of Phoenix, the largest for-profit university in the US, bought BPP Holdings, the UK's largest private higher education provider specialising in law, accounting and business (Fearn, 2009). Apollo used the acquisition to expand into Europe and while this expansion was successful, US operations became enmeshed in funding turmoil and lawsuits instigated by the US government (The Telegraph, 2009). In 2016, shareholders of the Apollo Education Group agreed to a buyout of $1.14 billion from a group including private-equity firm Apollo Global Management (Armental, 2016; Business Wire, 2016). Future plans are presently unclear.

r. *UK-based Montagu buying UK-based College of Law, which became the University of Law, 2012, then selling it to Amsterdam-based GUS, 2015*

The private equity firm Montagu bought the College of Law for £200m in 2012 (Rayner, 2012). From a strategic point of view, private equity sought to take advantage of educational deregulation in the UK, which allowed the previously not-for-profit College of Law to substantially restructure. The College of Law was subsequently renamed the University of Law (Pingal & Cook, 2012). Montagu sold the University of Law after it became clear that generating the desired levels of profitability was more difficult than expected. In June 2015 the University of Law announced that it had been acquired by the Global University Systems BV (GUS), an educational aggregator that originated in the for-profit London School of Business and Finance (Kalia, 2015). Under this new structure, the University of Law will continue to operate as a distinct educational institution.

s. *US-based Capella buys UK-based RDI, 2011, renames it Arden University and sells it to GUS in 2016*

RDI was established in 1990 in the UK as a distance-learning provider. In 2011 Capella, a US-based accredited provider of distance learning, acquired RDI to accelerate its international expansion (Capella, 2011; Stych, 2011). The strategy did not come to fruition and in 2016 Global University Systems (GUS) acquired the by-now renamed Arden University (Global University Systems, 2016; Morgan, 2016)).

t. *US-based Laureate buys 80 schools and sells Swiss hospitality and business schools Les Roches and Glion in 2016*

Laureate, a network of globally operating higher education institutions, aims to balance local managerial autonomy with scaled network benefits through centralised marketing, shared curricula, faculty, degree programmes and student exchange opportunities. To enhance and further enrich these offerings, Laureate built a network of about 80 schools globally between 1999 and 2016. In March 2016 Laureate and Eurazeo, a leading hospitality investment company, signed an agreement for the transfer of ownership of Les Roches and Glion hospitality and business schools (Laureate, 2016). The primary driver for the sale appeared to be Laureate's desire to reduce debt prior to its initial public offering, which took place in January 2017.

If traditional business school providers may view the acquisition of a university as something unusual, acquiring universities is something that for-profit educational providers understand very well. Whatever the original mission of a university may have been and whatever announcements are made by the acquirer promising continuity and the sacrosanct nature of the original institution, there is little evidence that this is true. The goal of the for-profit, after all, is to make profit. Attempts to do so are made through the introductions of new products and programmes, new geographies and the consolidation of costs.

Summary and Conclusions

No doubt further examples can be cited and glaring omissions have been made in the above attempt to come to terms with the size, dynamism and volume of mergers and acquisitions within the recent business school landscape. The goal has been to highlight that change, even among many long-established and accredited business schools, is a regular occurrence and is thus something that not only business school deans but also regulators and accreditors need to think about.

Whether through the mergers of schools supported by chambers of commerce or individual or regional university consolidation or the buy-and-build strategies of recent market entrants such as GUS, there is clearly a move to size and scale. In a globalised business education market, building a global brand for a business school is a big job. Not all schools seek to expand their international awareness and recruitment — some will be able to prosper on a regional basis with strong local support — but more schools will realise that size is the prize even if the journey to that destination is a difficult one involving mergers, acquisitions and the pain of change.

References

Aalto University. (2016, January 20). *History of Aalto university*. Retrieved from http://www.aalto.fi/en/about/history

Anderson, L. (2008, January 9). Henley and Reading university reveal merger plans. *Financial Times*. Retrieved from https://www.ft.com/content/7aaf8dd8-beaf-11dc-8c61-0000779fd2ac

Armental, M. (2016, May 6). Apollo education shareholders approve $1.14 billion buyout. *The Wall Street Journal*. Retrieved from http://www.wsj.com/articles/apollo-education-shareholders-approve-1−14-billion-buyout-1462574658

Bradshaw, D. (2004, December 4). Hult takes over Huron. *Financial Times*. Retrieved from https://www.ft.com/content/a3adf99a-a280-11dc-81c4-0000779fd2ac

Bradshaw, D. (2013, May 2). Melbourne Business School wins merger battle with university. *Financial Times.* Retrieved from. https://www.ft.com/content/9ce7907a-b270-11e2-8540-00144feabdc0

Bradshaw, D. (2013, August 26). Meet the dean: Frank Bostyn, Rouen/Reims. *Financial Times.* Retrieved from https://www.ft.com/content/e8bcfe6a-08c2-11e3-ad07-00144feabdc00

Brown, R. (2014, November 25). *Index of colleges and universities that have closed, merged, or changed names [Blog post].* Retrieved from https://collegehistorygarden.blogspot.sg/2014/11/index-of-colleges-and-universities-that.html

Buckridge, C. (2009). Proposed merger will create a business and economics power-house at Melbourne. (2009, July 31). *The Melbourne Newsroom.* Retrieved from http://newsroom.melbourne.edu/news/n-96

Business Wire. (2016, February 8). Apollo Education Group, Inc. to be taken private in $1.1 billion transaction. *BusinessWire.* Retrieved from http://www.businesswire.com/news/home/20160208005571/en/Apollo-Education-Group-Private-1.1-Billion-Transaction

Capella. (2011, July 15). *Capella Education Company acquires Resource Development International Ltd* [News Release]. Retrieved from http://www.capellaeducation.com/investor-relations/investor-news/news-release-details/2011/Capella-Education-Company-Acquires-Resource-Development-International-Ltd/default.aspx

Clark, P. (2014). A struggling business school's long, strange saga gets another twist. *Bloomberg*, July 8.

Cornell. (2016, January 30). Cornell to establish an integrated College of Business. *Cornell Chronicles.* Retrieved from http://news.cornell.edu/stories/2016/01/cornell-establish-integrated-college-business

Econostrum.info. (2013, June). *When Euromed management became Kedge business School.* Retrieved from http://www.marseille.fr/newslettereco/jsp/site/Portal.jsp?document_id=241&portlet_id=18

Fearn, H. (2009, August 4). Apollo completes BPP takeover. *Times Higher Education.* Retrieved from https://www.timeshighereducation.com/news/apollo-completes-bpp-takeover/407663.article

Fraguerio, F., & Thomas, H. (2011). *Strategic leadership in the business school: Keeping one step ahead.* Cambridge, UK: Cambridge University Press.

Global University Systems. (2016, August 19). Global university systems announces acquisition of Arden university. *PR Newswire.* Retrieved from http://www.prnewswire.com/news-releases/global-university-systems-announces-acquisition-of-arden-university-590690651.html

Gluyas, R., & Trounson, A. (2009, October 1). Old boys scuttle Melbourne Business School merger with Mebourne University. *The Australian.* Retrieved from http://www.news.com.au/finance/work/old-boys-scuttle-melbourne-business-school-merger-with-melbourne-university/news-story/40cc33f36ef61847eaa81effc284fe20

Guilhon, A. (2015). Skema — The story of a merger. *Global Focus, 9*(3).

Hall, W. (2004). Bigger promises to be better: Manchester Merger: The new Manchester Business School should have more stability and clout but it still seeks more autonomy, writes William Hall: London. *The Financial Times*. 22 November.

Hult News. (2015). *Era of big B-school mergers extends networks for MBA students [Business Because]. [Blog Post]*. Retrieved from http://www.hult.edu/news/business-school-mergers-extends-networks-for-mba-students-ashridge-merger/

IE University. (2017). *Our story: Who we are*. Retrieved from https://www.ie.edu/university/about/who-we-are/

Independent Online. (2011, January 20). *The new dean of Henley Business School talks to Michael Prest about the future of business education*. The Independent Online. Retrieved from http://www.independent.co.uk/student/career-planning/vocational-study/professor-john-board-economics-has-a-lot-to-say-about-the-world-2189028.html

Kalia, J. (2015, June 2). Having lost two magic circle clients, University of Law sold to GUS less than three years after purchase. *Legal Business*. Retrieved from http://www.legalbusiness.co.uk/index.php/lb-blog-view/4230-having-lost-two-magic-circle-clients-university-of-law-sold-to-gus-less-than-three-years-after-purchase

Kedge Business School. (2012, November 5). *BEM and Euromed management to merge to create KEDGE Business School*. PR *Newswire*. Retrieved from http://www.prnewswire.com/news-releases/bem-and-euromed-management-merge-to-create-kedge-business-school-177247071.html

Kelly, S. (2016, February 3). 'Business College of the Future' will retain schools' identities. *Cornell Chronicles*. Retrieved from http://news.cornell.edu/stories/2016/02/business-college-future-will-retain-schools-identities

Laureate. (2016, March 15). *Agreement between Laureate Education, Inc. and Eurazeo for the sale of Glion and Les Roches hospitality management schools.* Retrieved from http://www.laureate.net/NewsRoom/PressReleases/2016/03/Agreement-between-Laureate-Education-Inc-and-Eurazeo

Lindsay, T. (2015, November 28). More US colleges poised to go bankrupt, according to three new studies. *Forbes*. Retrieved from www.forbes.com/sites/tomlindsay/2015/11/28/three-new-studies-more-u-s-colleges-poised-to-go-bankrupt/#1ac616b25b2f

Mitchell, N. (2015, November 25). Big is beautiful for merging universities. *BBC News*. Retrieved from http://www.bbc.com/news/business-34902884

Morgan, J. (2016, August 19). Arden university sold to global university systems. *Times Higher Education*. Retrieved from https://www.timeshighereducation.com/news/arden-university-sold-global-university-systems

Nguyen, P. (2015). What happens when business schools merge: A case study. *Journal of Business Case Studies (JBCS)*, *11*(4), 152.

Pettigrew, A. M., Cornuel, E., & Hommel, U. (2014). *The institutional development of business schools*. Oxford: Oxford University Press.

Pingal, S., & Cook, C. (2012, April 18). Montagu to buy legal education provider. *Financial Times*. Retrieved from https://www.ft.com/content/57067376-88ac-11e1-9b8d-00144feab49a

Potter, A. (2005). University of Sydney to withdraw from AGSM joint venture. *University of Sydney News*, 11 November 2005. Retrieved from http://sydney.edu.au/news

Rayner, J. (2012, April 17). College of Law sold in £200m private equity deal. *The Law Society Gazette*. Retrieved from https://www.lawgazette.co.uk/news/college-of-law-sold-in-200m-private-equity-deal/65199.fullarticle

Smith, E. (2012, January 20). BEM and Euromed in planned merger. *Financial Times*. Retrieved from https://www.ft.com/content/32573bbc-429a-11e1-97b1-00144feab49a

Stych, E. (2011, July 15). Capella buys U.K. online school. *Minneapolis/ St. Paul Business Journal*. Retrieved from http://www.bizjournals.com/twincities/news/2011/07/15/capella-buys-uk-online-school.html

The Telegraph. (2009, June 8). *BPP sold to Apollo for £303.5m*. Retrieved from http://www.telegraph.co.uk/finance/newsbysector/supportservices/5474584/BPP-sold-to-Apollo-for-303.5m.html

TiasNimbas Business School. (2009, October 8). *The Economist*. Retrieved from http://www.economist.com/node/14585227

Tienari, J., Aula, H., & Aarrevaara, T. (2016). Built to be excellent? The Aalto university merger in Finland. *European Journal of Higher Education*, 6(1), 25–40.

Tomazin, F. (2009, October 1). Melbourne Uni drops business school plan. *The Sydney Morning Herald*. Retrieved from http://www.smh.com.au/national/melbourne-uni-drops-business-school-plan-20090930-gcrg.html

Wanot, M. (2015, November 2). *CEIBS acquires Lorange Institute of Business Zurich*. [EFMD Blog] Retrieved from https://www.efmd.org/blog/view/725-ceibs-lorange-institute-of-business-zurich

Wiles, R., & Ryman, A. (2014). ASU finalizes agreement to integrated Thunderbird school. *AZCentral*, Part of the USA Today Network. Retrieved from http://www.azcentral.com

Chapter 8

Conclusion and Implications

Introduction

The last few decades have witnessed the tremendous growth and success of business schools around the world. Much of this growth can be attributed to the development of a global economy that has raised interest in and demand for management education and an on-going interest in business degrees at all levels. In this way, a business-oriented marketplace has fuelled the growth of business schools in every part of the world. While growth has provided a great financial opportunity for business educators of all types, the landscape is beginning to change and there will be significant disruption for many of the traditional business education providers (Bennis & O'Toole, 2005).

Just as business scholars study the shifts in industries and comment on the disruptive effects of technology and globalisation, as business educators we must look at our own industry and institutions and prepare for what lies ahead. New business models have fundamentally changed retailers, travel providers and telecommunications firms. Given rising costs, alternative delivery options and increasing competition, the business model for business school education is now also in question (Fragueiro & Thomas, 2011). It is time for business school scholars to look in the mirror and examine a realistic future for ourselves.

As Gary Hamel (2012) has suggested, we have the potential to be "map makers in an earthquake zone." At our cosy academic conferences, we discuss the need for change, point at all the signals and suggest that we re-think the very nature of our industry but then go back to work to count our citations, teach our courses and manage our programmes. And what do we teach? Ironically, we teach the successes and failures of management and show students the failure of Kodak to see the change in the photography market as the world quickly shifted from film to digital. Yet we continue to operate within our own paradigms of higher education that necessitates research, classrooms and physical institutions.

The "pressure points" of competition – escalating fees, demographic changes and consumer concerns over the value proposition of business degrees are evident in Western markets. In Eastern markets demand is high at the moment, although supply – and certainly high-quality supply – is insufficient. Albeit for different reasons in the west and in the east, the traditional model for business schools is being called into question and is ready for disruption (Lorange, 2008).

In some industries, notably in the consumer-facing sectors mentioned above – retail, travel and telecommunications – fundamental shifts have taken place as an entire industry has been revolutionised by a new platform ecosystem, a concept that has garnered new awareness in recent years as digital disruption has become commonplace (Van Alstyne, Parker, & Choudary, 2016).

Perhaps it is time for a platform disruption aimed at the fundamentals surrounding the paradigm of business school education? Developing a service orientation would require a new platform that takes control of determining course and programme content away from faculty in favour of a more student-centric approach. A novel approach to student-based learning is underway at Boston University's Questrom School of Business in the US (Carlile, Davidson, Freeman, Thomas, & Venkatraman, 2016). The new Master of Science in Management Studies (MSMS) programme embraces "partner-based learning" and moving the centre point of programme design from faculty to the needs of the students.

However, business schools, rather than properly considering a new platform ecosystem or overall business model, seem to be locked in a stalemated "spending war" as the need for differentiation spurs increases in a "country club level" of facility investments, proliferation of marketing and a resulting increase in prices for programmes at all levels. In many ways, business schools have become a big business as the demand for degrees and management education continues to grow. Yet, there are some fundamental questions about the future of the current business school business model.

Too often, as inward-looking academics set the norms for faculty expectations and institutional leadership, business schools act and operate like a closed guild rather than as independent competitors. To better understand and illustrate the challenges implicit in the current business school model, this final chapter examines the fundamental value propositions and value chains associated with various programme and business school types.

Value Chains and Value Proposition

Throughout, this book has considered business school using a view of the value chains of the various offerings. This analysis of value chains has highlighted a number of unique considerations as well as the wide-ranging differences in the offerings between programme types. With each of the programmes, schools must: find students; house and feed students; teach students; provide space; provide technology; offer career services; and manage alumni. The value chain highlights not only the complexity of each of the programmes but also the potential range of services. While there are vast differences by country, strategic grouping and portfolio of an institution, there are a number of trends that are contributing toward the likelihood of potential disruption:

- *Marketing of programmes* — the globalisation of business schools has put significant emphasis on both the traditional and online marketing of programmes both domestically and internationally. Even smaller institutions are feeling the pressure to build global awareness to maximise the number and quality of students who apply. Anecdotally, marketing budgets, as a proportion of overall school sales, range from 3% or 4% of the top line to a jaw-dropping 25% to 30%. To help gain leverage in the global competitive landscape, many schools use professional agents to help market their programmes, especially in large and complex markets such as Asia, Africa and Latin America. In addition to advertising and global reach, schools are also spending significant time and resources to improve their ranking results. The costs associated with marketing and optimising student intakes across all levels of programmes continue to escalate.
- *Housing differences* — as the cost of business school programmes has increased in recent years so too have the expectations of students and investment in housing by business schools. Traditional dormitories *may* suffice for undergraduate programmes but the quality expectations for MBA and other graduate students are at an entirely different level. Of course, executive education is in a completely separate league as business schools find the need to run executive conference centres to attract students and corporate clients. Many executive education administrators know only too well that a poor experience with housing or meal services can kill a reputation faster than any inferior learning experience in the classroom.
- *Facilities, spaces and technology provisions* — along with basic dormitories the old days of traditional classrooms with simple chalkboards

and a library full of books are long gone from competitive business schools. Unique study spaces, separate graduate or MBA lounges, high-tech classrooms and leading technology applications are now minimum essentials. This not only adds costs but also creates challenges in separating and managing the various segments of students and their campus experience.

- *Traditional, local mind-set* — business schools are often focused on their local or regional marketplace for admissions, career services and business partnerships. Yet a globally connected world requires a global mind-set that breaks down the barriers of geography. Business school deans must take a global view and consider how they might play in a new platform that may soon be redefined.

While these trends in the value chains of business schools may have an impact on the strategic actions of an institution, it is important to recognise that the portfolio of programmes may provide a different level of emphasis in some areas. Most business schools offer a variety of programmes from undergraduate to PhD with a predominate focus on the MBA suite of programmes and the associated rankings. While the portfolio of programmes may vary, there are clear global trends across the general programme types.

- *Undergraduate* — while this continues to be a strong offering on a global basis, some countries are facing changing demographics. As a result, many schools are looking to attract more foreign students (at full fees) and considering ways of differentiating their programmes. Competition for top undergraduate students continues to be intense. In fact, there is much debate about the value of a four-year degree (US model) versus a three-year degree (UK model) at the undergraduate level and the role that undergraduate education plays in society (Colby, Ehrlich, Beaumont, & Stephen, 2003).
- *Pre-experience master's* — these programmes are a growing trend, emerging from European schools as an alternative to the MBA. Such programmes are perceived by potential students as having a lower opportunity cost or as a way of jump-starting careers. Many schools are also starting to use these programmes as an add-on to undergraduate programmes to not only create an attractive offering but also enhance revenue from the same base of students.
- *MBA* — there is a declining level of global interest in the traditional two-year full-time MBA programme. This puts pressure on some schools to continue growth or even maintain levels in their MBA

programmes. While MBA programmes still generally offer good revenue and healthy margins, it is only a matter of time before it does not make sense for some schools to continue this degree offering.

- *EMBA* – programme expectations from potential students are high. Finding students willing to pay the high fees and take on an MBA programme at the executive level is challenging. While many companies used to sponsor their employees, this practice has been under pressure in recent years. A growing trend is a partnership EMBA model where multiple schools work together to not only deliver the programme but also build global cohorts).
- *Executive education* – schools are facing unprecedented competition not only from each other but also from consultancies, training providers and on-line educators. Most business schools are seeing flat or declining revenues from executive education. Access to information online or from other sources is certainly raising questions about the value of some executive programmes though some schools often find opportunities for specialisation in executive education offerings based on faculty strengths or unique partnerships.

Demand for each of these programme types grew over recent decades and to capture the potential revenue, many universities launched several new programme types including full-time MBA, part-time MBA, specialised master's programmes, open enrolment executive programmes, customised executive programmes and others. Now that the demand for management education is softening in many markets, debate is focussed on new revenue models. As the competition increases and demand shifts, it is time for business schools genuinely to evaluate their portfolio of programmes and develop a strategic view based on their unique situation.

Revenue Implications and Strategic Groups

As highlighted throughout this book, a tension between the traditional university model of advancing knowledge and the more recent phenomenon of providing management education that carries a promise of return on investment has raised fundamental questions about the revenue model of business schools.

One of the traditional sources of revenue for many schools is government funding. Whether this is in the form of direct or indirect support of student fees, many schools, including the for-profit institutions, are large users of this type of national funding. Governments have long recognised the link between an educated workforce and economic growth. Around the world, public funding accounts for more than 50% of university funding while this figure is around 75% in OECD countries (OECD, 2010). However, as state and regional governments face fiscal problems, funding for educational institutions has become strained in the face of rising numbers of students.

While government funding may provide significant financial support for university education in some cases, business schools have also relied on an increasing rate of student tuition fees for both undergraduates and postgraduates. Over the past 15 years, while income levels for universities have remained largely constant, tuition fees for universities in the US have increased tremendously, shifting from government subsidies to tuition hikes. It is projected that by 2020 the fees for a traditional four-year undergraduate degree will reach $330,000 (Taylor, 2010). The same is true for MBA programmes, which may charge in excess of $100,000 per year. This rapidly increasing price tag for business education creates an affordability divide and calls into question the value of many programmes, especially, the MBA. In essence, students' "Willingness-to-pay" very high tuition fees is continuously being questioned.

Other funding sources for business schools typically involve fundraising from alumni or external partners. While alumni donations and grant sponsorship are more common in the US, other institutions around the world are working to build endowments through fundraising. The fundamental financial sustainability of the business school model is a serious question for many institutions. While the sources and size of revenue for business schools have become critical factors for their future outlook, relatively few schools link their revenue orientation into the management of their faculty. In other words, the measurement and management of faculty continue to centre on publication counts and so on. This effort is not always aligned with the interests of the paying customer (the student).

Chapter 4 outlined a potential model called a "revenue-delivered view" of faculty teaching contributions. This approach, not unlike those used in consulting firms, may provide an opportunity to move towards a "common currency" in considering the contributions of faculty in teaching. By performing some simple calculations using revenue/student/course, we can quickly discern the levels of revenue supported by individual faculty members. (Ironically, the lack of alignment between school-level revenue goals and the faculty-level measures are substantially at odds with our own teaching on cascading management objectives and enterprise performance management!)

While revenue delivered may only be one factor related to faculty contributions, it seems to be a missing part of the equation in business schools today. Alignment on revenue can help significantly with faculty allocations across different activities. It is up to each institution to consider its own differentiated competitive position in the marketplace, though surely these decisions are more fruitful if they are evidence-based.

As the future of management education becomes more uncertain, business schools would be well served to consider their strategic positioning and portfolio plans. The strategic options are different depending on the nature of the business school. We have argued that three strategic groups emerge due to the nature of governance and brand reputation: *publicly funded, elite* and *private* business schools.

The *publicly funded* schools are the most common yet are the most financially limited form of business school. In addition to regulations and governance by the state, these schools are typically part of a larger university system and may not operate with much autonomy. The publicly funded schools are often more affected by declining MBA enrolments and executive education demand. As such, we will likely see more schools in this strategic group focus increasingly on boosting volume through strong undergraduate programmes and the creative use of digital platforms or alliance structures.

The *elite* business schools dominate the top-level rankings and have healthy endowments that allow them more strategic choices. They compete aggressively for top students with scholarships and the promise of their brand. One of the on-going activities in elite schools is the protection and use of the brand while also continuously building the endowment funds. Many of the elite schools are now working to improve their global reach and impact. Several have set up campuses in Asia or other regions while others are working through alliances. We expect that the elite schools will continue to strengthen their image as they find new opportunities for selective growth around the world.

Private institutions generally do not receive direct funding from the state but often do benefit from students who can afford higher fees and subsequently can make donations as alumni. With newer private entrants to the business school marketplace, longevity may be less secure. The options for this strategic group may be more limited than larger public schools and the well-endowed elite schools. The challenge for private schools is to find a clear market position based on location, brand and core competence. The pressure of competition is intense within each of these business school strategic segments. These broadly defined groups provide a rough basis for considering portfolio options on the strategic direction for each school.

While there are many factors to consider, it seems clear that offering "standard" programmes across most business schools is not sustainable in the long-term. Therefore, each school must take an objective view of its current strengths, market position and future demand to determine the portfolio that will provide competitive advantage. With a clear sense of a competitive portfolio, business schools would be well served to then consider how to drive innovation and evaluate the business model on which to deliver their offerings.

Driving Innovation or Changing the Business Model

The success and growth of business schools is due in part to the major shifts in our society as we grapple with an increasingly "VUCA" world where volatility, uncertainty, complexity and ambiguity have become the norm. These disruptions and trends continue to shape the future of management education teaching and require educators to rethink many of their leadership programmes and the curriculum of business.

As outlined in Chapter 6, managers in the future will require the contextual mastery to not only understand the nature of their internal organisation, but also the complexity of their external environment. In the future, leaders must move beyond understanding to even challenge the very nature of the businesses that they operate. To do this, business leaders of the future must have relationships at all levels and be able to work across cultures. Business today requires a high degree of behavioural complexity, not only to be self-aware but also able to flex their own style and needs to adjust to the situation at hand. Given the challenges inherent in business today, managers must have a high level of self-efficacy to take on difficult tasks and find new ways to "rise to the challenges" that today's dynamic business environment provides.

While there will be rapid acceptance of the VUCA world along with higher expectations of business leaders, the tradition and general acceptance of the age-old format of business schools has remained largely intact. In the new business environment of today and the future, we believe that management education will need to address the implications of several dilemmas as outlined in Chapter 6. The following seven dilemmas create tension in the business school system and we suggest that the choices that each business school makes will be a function of the strategic direction and choices based resources available, market competition, and the targeted customer segments. We review these seven dilemmas and offer areas of application for the future.

- *Individual and Organisation* – creating changes at the individual level cannot be accomplished without addressing changes at the organisation level. Therefore, management development must consider both the individual as well as the organisational context. This may be a fundamental shift in the approach that some schools make in executive education as well as postgraduate professional programmes.
- *Cognitive and Behavioural* – while this is often characterised as the balance between "hard" and "soft" skills that business leaders must possess, the combination of these competencies is often difficult to master. In this age of digitisation and analytics, business schools will work to not only craft the right balance but also find new pedagogical approaches to accelerate skill building and create potential differentiation in the marketplace by even creating options to customize the level of "Soft" skills based on career interests.
- *Action and Reflection* – in the classrooms we are often focused on the thinking and planning associated with strategic business topics, yet it is often the action (or inaction) that can actually make a difference between winning and losing. As educators, we may wish to consider how we train business leaders to develop patterns of action to aid in the execution (not just the thinking) of business plans. Application-oriented approaches may create new types of business school experiences or alternative pathways in curriculum to create more value for both students and employers.
- *Theory and Practice* – the divide between academic theory and practice is the subject of much debate and concern. Since theories are frequently quite general, we must find more ways to contextualise our theories and help managers learn to explore the application of management as both an art and a science. This may result in more business school focus by industry to help bring relevancy to the marketplace and harness unique resources that create competitive advantage. Schools may wish to consider a variation of programmes that offer more pragmatic skills as a way to link with specific employers in the region.
- *Teaching and Facilitation* – there are often multiple ways for students to learn and business educators are becoming more adept in determining the optimal approach. Business schools are taking a hard look

at their curriculums and approaches to rethink the balance between various inquiry-based learning and traditional teaching methods. Alternative modes of learning and pedagogy have not been widely contested since the advent of the case-teaching method. New learning approaches may challenge the value proposition of traditional educational models in business schools and proactive institutions may develop alternative pathways for experiencing learning objectives.

- *Intellectual and Emotional Experiences* – when business leaders are asked about experiences that shaped their careers, they often cite instances that extended beyond their intellectual and emotional comfort zones. These learning experiences are generally not from the classroom environment and pose a question to educators on how to create development experience that might stretch individuals as a part of the value of our programmes and offerings. In some programmes, a project-based capstone requirement can often challenge the emotional and professional development of students.
- *Formal and Informal Learning* – in the business school classroom we design learning with activities and other interventions with great intent, however informal learning on the job is often the best teacher. Blending the formal education goals with the reality of informal learning remains a goal of many business programmes, yet we often rely on traditional modes of classroom delivery. Perhaps it is time for business schools to create more shades of grey between the campus learning and workplace learning to maintain relevance and find new ways to create value.

The challenge of management education is indeed complex and multifaceted as we consider these dilemmas. Business schools and leaders in management education are often at odds in addressing these challenges as potential solutions may be different to the traditional paradigm that we have about "school" and "education". These dilemmas raise questions about who teaches or facilitates learning. Some of these educational approach questions also raise the question of qualification for teaching. Does the instructor need to be a PhD with the title of "Professor" to create a learning opportunity? Could great facilitators be recognised as educators? In addition to considering the skills and role of the teacher, educational institutions must also ask hard questions about the way we deliver our programmes.

How do we leverage our increasing virtual world to maximise the learning opportunity for our students? What if we eliminated the classroom as we know it today and re-invent learning environments to suit our purpose?

While we are raising questions, we must also reconsider the functional nature of most business schools organised by discipline. Could we take a lesson on how we might develop more dynamic capabilities by working in alternative structures? There are many more questions and it seems time that business school leaders work more actively and apply our own research methods and critical thinking to our own business.

In addition to considering internal innovations on how we might reinvent our models of education, it is also necessary that we consider the external competitive and alliance landscape in business education. With the rapid growth in business education followed by an uncertain future, we can expect to see some level of industry consolidation or combination. Some institutions find that they are in need of mergers for survival while others are looking for alliance partners to help create global capabilities. In Chapter 7 we highlight a number of recent merger activities in the industry. Many traditional business school leaders may view the alliance and merger activity of recent years as counter-cultural to the tradition of educational institutions. However, the business school industry is in many ways no different than other industry sector facing competitive pressures and changing business models.

As we move to a more globally connected network of schools in Australia, Asia, Africa, the Americas and Europe, we fully expect to see more strategic alliances and interesting combinations of business schools in the future.

Conclusions and Conjectures

We have explored the current state of business schools today with a genuine interest and vested position in their success in the future. Yet we hope we have objectively considered the current pressures and perceptions on the standard business model of the institutions today. As business school deans, we are not just concerned about the future – we are adamant that our industry is poised for significant disruption. While we study business change and offer advice to managers, we are not accustomed to taking our own medicine.

Rather than providing the answers with what comes next, we hope this book has provided a call to action. As educators, we recognise that we are immersed in our own system and may not have an externally objective view. Yet it is critical that we not only work to innovate, to create a new future but also potentially disrupt, even cannibalise, our current business model.

Ideas and breakthroughs often come from the fringes of a system, rather than from within R&D labs, and this may also be true in considering our future. As we see the exciting development of Asia and now Africa perhaps a new platform for management development will take shape. Moving to a new platform such as a digital mode would certainly be painful for those who have made significant brick and mortar investments — try explaining that to your board of trustees after spending hundreds of millions of dollars on your campus!

As academics, we expect to see more studies, more experiments and more theories on the future models of education. While education models and practices continue to evolve, we must be sure to stay anchored with the original intent of business schools as stated by the Ford and Carnegie Foundation Studies of 1959 — namely, to professionalise management.

Our future transformation lies before us yet our vision of the future is still unclear and uncertain. We recognise that we cannot wait for the fog to clear, as it will be too late. As business school leaders, we must take steps forward to innovate, experiment and try new models of delivering on our promise. We hope that by the time this book is published we are already taking forward steps in our journey. After all, we owe this to our profession as stewards of the science.

References

Bennis, W. G., & O'Toole, J. (2005). How Business Schools lost their way. *Harvard Business Review*, *83*(5), 96–104, 154.

Carlile, P., Davidson, S., Freeman, K., Thomas, H., & Venkatraman, N. (2016). *Reimagining business education: Insights and actions from the business education jam*. Bingley: Emerald Publishing Limited.

Colby, A., Ehrlich, T., Beaumont, E., & Stephen, J. (2003). *Educating citizens: Preparing America's undergraduates for lives of moral and civic responsibility* (Vol. 6). New York, NY: John Wiley & Sons.

Fragueiro, F., & Thomas, H. (2011). *Strategic leadership in the business school: Keeping one step ahead*. Cambridge, UK: Cambridge University Press.

Hamel, G. (2012). What matters now. *Strategic Direction*, *28*(9). Bingley: Emerald Group Publishing Limited.

Lorange, P. (2008). *Thought leadership meets business: How business schools can become more successful*. Cambridge, UK: Cambridge University Press.

OECD. (2010). Tertiary graduation and entry rates. *OECD Factbook 2010: Economic, Environmental and Social Statistics* (pp. 182–183). OECD Publishing.

Taylor, M. (2010). *Crisis on campus: A bold plan for reforming our colleges and universities.* Toronto: Knopf Doubleday Publishing.

Van Alstyne, M. W., Parker, G. G., & Choudary, S. P. (2016). Pipelines, platforms, and the new rules of strategy. *Harvard Business Review, 94*(4), 54–62.

Index